CLEAN HANDS SAVE LIVES

THIERRY CROUZET

CLEAN HANDS SAVE LIVES

TRANSLATION THOMAS CLEGG

tcrouzet.com

(cc) by-nc-nd, 2014, L'Âge d'Homme, Thierry Crouzet & Thomas Clegg
L'Âge d'Homme, CP 5076, 1002 Lausanne (Suisse)
5, rue Férou, 75006 Paris (France)

www.lagedhomme.com

MAKE A DONATION

The author cedes his rights to the Clean Hands Save Lives Fund created by Didier Pittet under the auspices of the Fondation Philanthropia – CleanHandsSave-Lives.org. Each time you buy a copy of this book you are giving a doctor, a nurse, a healthcare officer, or a first-aid worker in disadvantaged countries a bottle of alcohol-based handrub[1] and thereby saving lives. Our publisher, Editions L'Âge d'Homme, also supports this initiative.

FOREWORD

When the implications of the work of the 19th century pioneers in hospital infection—such as Semmelweis, Nightingale, and Lister—were fully understood they were seen as a revolution in health care safety practices. It would be inconceivable to those pioneers that patients in the 21st century would still be dying from infections related to their care. Indeed, they would be truly shocked to learn that the underlying problem of cleanliness continues to be the source of infections in modern hospitals. Yet, around the world, people die or become ill in hospitals every day because they are exposed to bacteria carried on the hands of those who are caring for them.

Clean Care is Safer Care was the very first Global Patient Safety Challenge started by the World Health Organization (WHO) as part of its inaugural program of patient safety initiated in response to the World Health Assembly Resolution 55.18 in 2002. A key element of the Global Challenge was the commitment to improve hand hygiene. Clean hands became the Challenge's most visible goal, and this approach resonated with patients and families, clinicians and managers, health ministers and journalists.

Experts and scientists worldwide came together to produce a comprehensive set of evidence-based hand hygiene guidelines and the Challenge was embraced throughout the WHO's regions with great enthusiasm and commitment.

There was innovation too. The introduction of alcohol-based handrubs was shown to be more effective than soap and water. More importantly, its use overcame the lack of easy access to a sink, or in hospitals in poorer countries, to any water supply at all.

Successful global programs require great leadership. This book is about restoring the value and virtues of cleanliness firmly established by Florence Nightingale all those years ago. It is about showing how a world committed to health care can embrace a positive change. It is about how lives can be saved. Most of all, it is about how a great leader can inspire, galvanize action, transform existing practices and sustain the benefit of changes.

This book is the story of how one leader, Didier Pittet, successfully realized his dream of saving lives through clean hands worldwide, with the support of the WHO.

It is about how he brought his skill, his experience, his academic rigor and his generosity, honed and developed in the hospitals of Geneva, Switzerland, to serve patients and families around the world. Few are aware of his contribution or even know his name, but many owe their health and their lives to him.

WHO is fortunate that Didier Pittet said "yes" when the call went out for his help. We are grateful for his exemplary leadership and for the bonds that he has helped us to forge with health systems and academic institutions around the world to make care safer. Much can be learned from the story told so well and so inspirationally in this book. It deserves a wide readership.

Dr. Margaret Chan,
Director-General,
World Health Organization

Sir Liam Donaldson,
Patient Safety Envoy,
World Health Organization

A hospital bed is a parked taxi with the meter running.

Groucho Marx

One of the cafés had that brilliant idea of putting up a slogan: 'the best protection against infection is a good bottle of wine', which confirmed an already prevalent opinion that alcohol is a safeguard against infectious disease.

Albert Camus, *The Plague*, 1947[2]

PROLOG
MODEST MEASURE, BIG EFFECT

Mid-March 2012, I receive an unexpected phone call from Geneva. "I just met the most extraordinary doctor!" my friend Geneviève cries. She is speaking loudly, brimming with enthusiasm, emotion choking her usually hoarse voice. "He's incredible. You must write about his life. The Queen of England dubbed him Commander of the British Empire, but nobody knows him, not even here in Switzerland. He's on the list of Nobel Peace Prize candidates. A professor of medicine who saves millions of lives every year."

A month later, I find myself seated opposite Didier Pittet, an athletic fifty year old with a passing resemblance to Indiana Jones. His amber eyes still dappled with sunlight, he has just come back from Afghanistan, where he spent ten days visiting the country's hospitals as a delegate from the World Health Organization.[3]

Although Didier is supposed to be explaining his work to me, in his head he is still in the stark light of Central Asia. In a voice that is sometimes serious, sometimes filled with laughter, he tells me about his journey.

Didier is wearing jeans, hiking boots, and a backpack, with a large wheeled suitcase trailing along behind him. He is walking through a narrow concrete maze beside his friend, Professor Kurt-Wilhelm Stahl, a retired doctor and biochimist who devotes his efforts to treating leishmaniasis,[4] a common skin disease in Afghanistan.

The sun is approaching its zenith. In the stifling heat, Didier and Kurt-Wilhelm leave Gate 1 of the NATO military base at Mazar-i-Sharif, not far from the border with Uzbekistan. Two gray walls over four meters tall and topped with barbed wire hem them in. Above their heads floats a hot-air balloon loaded with radar equipment. Planes and helicopters crisscross the sliver of visible sky. In some areas, wire fencing used in place of the concrete walls allows them a glimpse of Gate 2, three kilometers away. Their backpacks and the suitcase start to weigh upon them as do the gazes of soldiers stationed in the watchtowers. However, complaining is out of the question. Afghanistan has been at war for more than thirty years.

Didier thinks of his children, his family. Once again, he has abandoned them, using up vacation time to travel around the world doing volunteer work. "So you won't be spending Easter with us," his wife Séverine said reproachfully before he left. Didier replied that the Afghans needed his help. His repeated absences may have cost him his first marriage, but he feels no guilt.

The previous evening, when the Airbus used by the German Luftwaffe to transport NATO troops made a stopover for the night at the Termez military base in Uzbekistan, Didier found himself face-to-face with a WHO poster, a sort of comic strip page in black-and-white, drawn in a clean-line style. The illustration was of two hands clasped together, fingers interlaced. NATO's graphic designers had replaced the official logo with their own, as if to say they'd adopted the message: "Save Lives: Clean Your Hands."

Little by little, all over the world, the idea is sinking in. Didier had already scientifically demonstrated this almost age-old truth. Now he needs to explain, train, and convince people of it. Every day, at least half a million patients are infected in hospitals, while 20 to 50,000 people die as a result of failing to follow an ostensibly simple practice.[5] "It's a silent pandemic," sums up Didier. With a gesture as simple as cleansing one's hands, it is possible to at least halve these numbers, reducing mortality in developing regions by 50 or even 75%.

Afghanistan is the 130th country to join the WHO's hand hygiene initiative.[6] Didier and Kurt-Wilhelm approach Gate 2, defended by Macedonian and Croatian soldiers in battle fatigues. They make Didier enter one stall, and Kurt-Wilhelm another. They search the two doctors. The backpacks are emptied, and then the suitcase, which is stuffed full of posters, brochures and, most preciously, small bottles of alcohol-based handrub. The miracle gel developed by Didier's team at HUG (Hôpitaux Universitaires de Genève—the teaching hospitals of the University of Geneva). It is a product we all discovered back in 2009, during the H1N1 flu epidemic.[7] It is now sold everywhere, having found its place in handbags, kitchens, schools, bathrooms, and globetrotters' backpacks. A few drops, twenty seconds of hand rubbing, and goodbye to viruses and bacteria. It's quicker and more effective than soap.

Thirty minutes later, Didier and Kurt-Wilhelm find themselves back in the overheated concrete maze, headed for Gate 3, under Afghan control.

"Are they going to search us again?" asks Didier.

"Don't you worry about that," Kurt-Wilhelm reassures him.

"The alcohol won't be a problem?"

"If our Afghan friends are there, everything will be fine."

Didier doesn't want to think about other possible outcomes. Instead, he reflects back on his morning. Having just disembarked from the troop transport with his eardrums still ringing, he was invited to visit the military base's hospital, an installation equipped with the most modern technology. Didier spoke with administrators, nurses, and doctors. He questioned patients. He looked at the radiography of a case of hepatic echinococcosis.[8] He was asked for advice. He promised to give a talk before his departure.

Didier likes hospitals. When he was younger and took on individual cases, he loved the actual human contact with patients. Like a sculptor working with clay, he literally took them into his hands. Through his fingers, he felt their life. Now, he experiences the same emotion with respect to hospitals. Didier has visited so many establishments, studied so many health systems that he has ended up acquiring a sixth sense. Hospitals have become his new patients.

But between him and the Mazar-i-Sharif hospital, there now stand two Afghans in black turbans, with bushy beards, crooked teeth, and assault rifles in their hands. These local soldiers remain steadfast in front of their sentry boxes. It is the last checkpoint. Beyond them, stretching all the way to the limits of the base, is a packed line of trucks, pickups, and a vast assortment of other vehicles. The drivers wait patiently, imperturbable beneath the sun, in the desert dust.

Kurt-Wilhelm presents the mission order. Other Afghan soldiers come forth. By reflex, Didier shows them his Swiss passport with the white cross on a red background, the symbol of the Red Cross reversed, held out like a talisman.

"Look! Faridullah and Ibrahim are here," Kurt-Wilhelm says happily as a pickup advances to take charge of them.

Didier is talkative. He abbreviates his technical explanations with words like "thing", "stuff", "doodad", etc. He praises Kurt-Wilhelm's enthusiasm fulsomely: "Fantastic, marvelous, extraordinary, brilliant." It is obvious that the man likes people. Didier extols the courage of Faridullah the dermatologist, and Ibrahim the young surgeon who, under the pretext of being an apprentice, does not even receive a salary.

I think of Steve Jobs, whose biography I just finished reading. I am facing someone who is every bit as exceptional. Didier Pittet is not only a top-notch scientist and a doctor of world renown, but also a gifted communicator. Geneviève told me, "When they make a movie in Switzerland, they put 100% of the budget into production and 0% into promotion. And as a result, no one sees the film." But Didier has understood that proving the technical effectiveness of hand hygiene is not enough to make it a universal, enduring habit. The idea has to be promoted, giving everyone the opportunity to adopt it as their own.

Didier seems to me to be a visionary yet also politically astute, pragmatic yet perfectionist, intransigent yet charismatic, creative yet directive. A cocktail of character traits which at first sight seem contradictory, but when assembled together, engender outstanding human beings. This can no doubt be exhausting for the person's entourage—like Steve Jobs, Didier suffers from orthorexia—an obsession with eating correctly—and also living correctly, waking up correctly, thinking correctly. He's very ortho-something or other.

But the similarities with the founder of Apple end there. When, along with his team at HUG, Didier developed his alcohol-based handrub and the associated protocol for its use, he could have registered a patent, created a thriving company, and become a businessman worth millions. Instead, he decided to share his discovery and offer it to the whole of humanity. He showed us the direction the economy could take in the 21st century, an economy based on sharing rather than capitalization, an economy of peace rather than one of predation.

Steve Jobs was said to project a "reality distortion field": he would bewitch his audiences. Didier has a rather similar power. In less than four years, he was able to persuade over 15,000 hospitals to adopt his hand hygiene program. For my part, I allow myself to be charmed, touched, and moved by him. In my mind's eye, I join him in the disorderly warren of the Mazar-i-Sharif hospital, the only hospital in the northern region of Afghanistan, with all of 400 beds for eight million inhabitants.

Along with Kurt-Wilhelm, Didier observes the dermatological consultations in the leishmaniasis center. While subcutaneous injections are being administered, he helps a mother hold her six-year-old daughter with an infected thigh. The girl screams and cries. Then it's the turn of another, even younger, little girl with a lesion on her cheek. If she does not receive treatment as soon as possible, she'll be disfigured for life. Next is a teenaged boy, followed by a woman whose nose is being eaten away by the disease. Between attending to each patient, nurses rub their hands with the alcohol-based gel brought from Europe. Didier advises them and shows them the correct protocols, which are all the more vital as the hospital is cruelly lacking in supplies. There are few gloves, and needles must be re-used. The service only possesses one sterilizer, a model that has been prohibited for use in Western hospitals for thirty years now.

Further on, Didier discovers the obstetrics and gynecology clinic with its molding walls and damp, poorly aired and overcrowded rooms. Two to three women share a bed. Some of them are there to give birth, while others are waiting for an operation. Didier notices a few WHO posters about hand hygiene: it is a good thing. The more dilapidated the institution, the more disinfection becomes a critical issue. The patients' survival depends on it.

Hundreds of children overwhelm the pediatrics service. The neonatal service does not have any respirators. If a new-born child has to be intubated, the infant is doomed. There are eleven incubators, a quarter of them out-of-order, for sixteen newborns. The math is sadly easy to perform. There are sometimes three infants per incubator. There is only one sink, not easily accessible, and in any case there is no water. In these conditions, hand hygiene is impracticable. Bottles of alcohol-based gel would mitigate the problem, but there isn't enough of the product. The single nurse on duty, an American, speaks of countless fevers and infections. Each week, she witnesses tens of deaths.

In another overheated ward, eighteen children are being treated with their mothers next to them, often deeply religious Muslim women wearing blue burkas. The chief resident asks for advice from Didier, who examines X-ray results, in particular those of Siamese twins joined at their legs, who will probably never be separated. He examines some children, and the other mothers ask him to continue. Didier assures them that they are already in good hands, that they should trust their local doctor. A woman in a burka implores him to look at the child feeding at her breast. She approaches Didier and suddenly breaks taboo: in her eagerness to persuade him she lifts her veil, a gesture that could lead to her death by stoning as punishment. Didier hurriedly examines the child, and then all the others. And, each time, he rubs his hands with a few drops of the alcohol-based gel.

Didier leaves the pediatrics service, visits others, and the hospital itself becomes his privileged patient. There is no question of letting it down. In order to treat the ill, one needs first of all to treat the institution responsible for their care, overriding corruption and special interests. So Didier meets with the various academic, governmental, and religious authorities involved. In this respect, at least, he is lucky: "Hand hygiene is simple. Everyone understands about hands. We all learned from our mothers to wash up before eating. We're not inventing new scanners. And since I have nothing to sell, there's no money to take or to give. I'm simply there to help. So people listen to me. I explain how to produce alcohol locally, how to make the gel on a shoestring budget, from sugarcane and paraffin, for example."

As Didier tells me about his journey, I realize the scope of his work. I only have one desire: to ask him to tell me his entire life story. I want to know by what miracle he found himself at the convergence of human nature and science, how he came to understand that a gesture as simple as cleansing one's hands, repeated tirelessly, could save tens of thousands of lives each day. I want to find out what obstacles he's had to overcome,

22

what pitfalls he has avoided, what preconceptions he has had to fight. I sense in him the stubbornness of the mountain climber, an extreme perseverance, a greatness of soul, and a boundless generosity. I imagine that his initiative, in its very simplicity, has raised the hackles of the technocrats, the big pharmaceutical groups, and the international medical community. I realize above all that the hardest task still remains: making hand hygiene an everyday habit for each of us, and thereby saving an even greater number of lives. I need to learn more, to learn from one man's experience something that might be useful to us all.

CHAPTER I
WHEN HOSPITALS KILL

On 16 April 2013, the Canadian folk singer Rita MacNeil died at the age of 68 following post-surgical complications. The same day, a rumor began to spread on Internet and in the traditional media, blaming the tragedy on a nosocomial infection, or in other words, a disease contracted in hospital.

"The bugs patients catch while in care sicken 250,000 patients annually," wrote reporter André Picard in *The Globe and Mail*, "and kill between 8,000 and 12,000 Canadians. They are one of the leading causes of death in this country. [...] They kill twice as many people as breast cancer. [...] So why do we tolerate this? [...] In Canada, we are too closed-mouthed about problems in our health system."[9]

In the debate following the death of MacNeil, Robert Paterson declared on his blog: "Hospitals have become the most dangerous place you can be in today." He cited statistics from the California Department of Public Health revealing that "one in 20 hospital patients get infections. In California, roughly 200,000 people get hospital infections annually, and 12,000 of them die [...] That makes such infections one of the state's leading causes of death, ahead of automobile accidents."[10]

Throughout the United States, nosocomial infections kill 200,000 persons every year, the equivalent of a 747 airliner crashing every day, or a person dying every three minutes.[11] One might even agree with the French philosopher, Michel Foucault, that the hospital environment itself "creates disease by means of the enclosed, pestilential domain that it constitutes."[12]

A few hours after the announcement of Rita Mac-Neil's death, a press release denied that any nosocomial infection was a factor in her death. MacNeil was already seriously ill upon arrival at the hospital's emergency room and human error was ruled out as a contributing cause of death. But diagnoses are rarely as clearcut and convenient as officials suggest.

"I was returning to Paris on my motorcycle when I was struck head-on by a suitcase that had broken loose from a car," recalled actor and songwriter Guillaume Depardieu in his autobiography, *Tout donner*. "[...] Half of my leg was torn off, my shoulder was screwed up, and my arm was broken [...]."[13] On a freezing Saturday evening in 1995, Depardieu was admitted to the Raymond Poincaré Hospital in the Parisian suburb of Garches. Depardieu is a big fellow with a sad smile who would spend the next year of his life in the hospital, undergoing dozens of operations. The medical staff at Raymond Poincaré recommended reconstruction surgery for his right knee. "At the time," said Depardieu, "I was feeling good, I could walk. So I had mixed feelings about undergoing the procedure. It's weird, because I hesitated and I should have listened to my gut feeling."

The initial operation went well, but the knee reconstruction failed. Guillaume agreed to another procedure, replacing his damaged leg with a prosthesis in April 1996. "Obviously, when they put in a prosthesis, they have to take things out," he explained. "That involves operations they refer to as 'minor', which aren't as complicated as surgical reconstruction, but do require opening up the body and entail a risk of infection. And that's where, in my opinion, my troubles started."

After multiple surgeries, Guillaume Depardieu contracted two types of "golden staph".[14]

The bacteria were eating away at him from the inside. It felt like a carpenter was filing down his bones. A few years after the accident, the pain became so severe that Guillaume decided to have his leg amputated, even though he knew he would run the risk of the staphylococcus spreading to his brain, as in the case of French billionaire Jean-Luc Lagardère who died a week after a hip operation.[15]

Guillaume Depardieu survived. During his subsequent physical therapy, he was shocked to find himself meeting hundreds of other victims of nosocomial infections. "In fact, I discovered something much more serious than cinema. Since I'm always in need of battles, this became my new battle, the most important one, in terms of its urgency. Because there was a gulf—not even a gulf, but more of a whole parallel world—between what people knew about what was going on and what I was seeing and rubbing shoulders with."

He created the Guillaume Depardieu Foundation to collect testimony from the 770,000 French people who fall victim each year to nosocomial infections, of which 40,000 prove fatal.[16] "Within a year, everybody started to be afraid of hospitals and began to take a closer look: the figures are frightening," said Depardieu.[17] In a tragic twist of fate, in October 2008 Guillaume contracted pneumonia, along with a new infection by a methicillin-resistant golden staph (MRSA).[18] He died three days later.

A Chinese proverb says: "When you're ill, a good meal is worth more than a stay in hospital." The blogger Robert Paterson goes even further: "The first step would surely be to avoid surgery. [...] Much of surgery today is not vital. [...] But what if you have bad knees? [...] I was on my way to join this group myself. But since I lost 35 pounds, my knees are of course much better." His reasoning is irrefutable. Medical intervention is never as plain and simple as doctors like to suggest.

"They're eager to perform a triple heart-and-lungs transplant, forgetting a little too quickly that a few days later, the patient could be dying from a common infection caused by a poorly sterilized instrument," remarks Didier Pittet's wife, Séverine, a former communications officer for HUG and therefore familiar with the behavior of the medical profession.

Didier adds: "In Switzerland it's estimated that 70,000 people are affected each year by a nosocomial disease, with 2,000 patients dying as a result. Contrary to what one might imagine, these infections are not limited to exposure in hospitals. They can also be caught at the doctor's office or in an examining room. Studies show that intensive care units present the greatest risk of infection.[19] It is not so much the sector where one is treated that is responsible, but rather the condition of the patient. The weaker a person's natural defenses—and the more invasive the treatment provided—the greater the risk of developing a urinary tract infection (the most common type), pneumonia, or post-surgical complications."[20]

According to Didier Pittet, 50% of flu cases observed in hospitals are nosocomial.[21] This is because patients infect one another; because health care professionals are not systematically vaccinated; and because visitors bring viruses into hospitals.

Dozens of elderly patients succumb to nosocomial flu. One day, a young man confided to Didier: "Grandpa had to die of something, sooner or later." But for Didier, death always comes too soon, especially when it could be avoided by just a few simple gestures. "That man's grandfather could still be alive," says Didier with the quiet emotion of a doctor who will never become resigned to the death of a patient.

In the WHO's Burden of Diseases report on the primary causes of mortality,[22] nosocomial infections do not appear, due to the lack of reliable global statistics. "Statistics are complicated," explains Didier. "If a patient with prostate cancer has a heart attack and dies, what is the cause of death? When a leukemia patient dies of a nosocomial infection, the cause of death is registered as leukemia. Of course, leukemia made the patient vulnerable, but saying that it is the sole cause is inaccurate. According to our estimates,[23] nosocomial infections kill more than tuberculosis, malaria, and AIDS combined in any given year. In the West, these numbers represent 69 deaths per 100,000 inhabitants, a morbidity rate higher than lung cancer, making nosocomial infections the second most prevalent cause of death, tied with strokes."

2

Guillaume Depardieu paid with his life because of a medical fact doctors have long been aware of, starting with Francis Waldvogel, head of internal medicine[24] and the bacteriology laboratory at HUG. This Geneva University professor has spent his entire career fighting infections. Waldvogel's American peers have respectfully named the Swiss infection specialist "Mister Staph" in reference to his fundamental research on staphylococci. The HUG researcher derives a great deal of pride from this moniker and it gives him an unshakeable confidence that comes across in his authoritative manner.

In October 1983, Waldvogel welcomed a young Didier Pittet—who had just acquired his medical degree—into his service. He beheld a 26-year-old doctor with tousled brown hair and a piercing gaze. Didier first came to the Waldvogel's attention three years earlier, during a medical emergency in which they were both involved. "It was late afternoon," describes Waldvogel. "I was called to the bedside of a leukemia patient who wasn't doing well. I was surprised to see a fourth-year medical student accompanying the intern. Didier introduced me to the patient and then asked some pertinent questions. He showed a lot of courage by taking charge in this manner while just a student. I told myself: 'Here's a guy I need to keep my eye on.'"

In 1984, Waldvogel asked Didier what field he wanted to specialize in later on in his career.

"Intensive care, or hematology, perhaps..." Didier replied hesitantly.

"How about infectious diseases, does that tempt you?"

"You don't take first-year fellows. There are only senior physicians on your team."

"For you, there might be an exception. Think about it."

Didier meanwhile rotated through the required services—pneumology, cardiology, nephrology — working with all the professors.

Waldvogel continued to watch over him, and encourage him. Didier did not harbor any preconceived notions about his career. Nothing in his family background suggested a predisposition towards medicine, other than his parents' wish to see their son succeed in his studies. Didier's father, Robert, was a master electrician in Petit-Lancy,[25] a suburb of Geneva. Didier's mother, Fernande, left law school when her son was born in 1957 to care for the boy and manage the family's electrical shop. The Pittets had to sell their tiny Fiat 500 Topolino to buy a stroller for their infant son.

At the beginning of the 20th century, Didier's paternal grandparents were peasants who had settled in Petit-Lancy at the beginning of the 20th century. His maternal grandfather was a sort of working-class dandy, employed by the local electric company. His wife, an energetic woman from Austria who had also lived for a while in Zurich, opened a fashionable open-air café to which Genevans flocked in their hundreds to enjoy the *boules de Bâle sauce ravigote*, little sausages made of pork and smoked lard, with mustard and mayonnaise.

Didier's grandmother dreamt of living on the shores of Lake Geneva. Eventually she bought a field overlooking the lake's Left Bank, on the French side of the border in Chens-sur-Léman. Each night, she left her café well after midnight, sometimes as late as four in the morning. She would get on her Solex motorbike and—come rain, wind, or even snow,—she rode twenty kilometers to the house she had built on this site. Rather than falling exhausted into bed, she watered her flowers, tended her garden, and never allowed herself more than five or six hours of sleep. The next afternoon she would take the same route back, admiring the lake's dazzling waters. "She lived to work," Didier says. "My mother called her a vulture. She was a penny pincher, but nonetheless, she got along with everyone."

Didier was born into this modest family with strong personalities, attached to the land around Petit-Lancy. "He was an extremely sensitive child," says Brigitte Pittet-Cuénod, his first wife, who married Didier in September 1983 just before he entered Waldvogel's service. "My former mother-in-law often told me that Didier cried a lot. Because other children were making fun of him, he once threw his glasses into a stream. His father was a plain, righteous man, a classic *pater familias* endowed with natural authority, the big chief and the source of all wisdom. He liked sports and pushed Didier to surpass himself. 'Stop whining and second-guessing yourself, and go for it!' One can still detect a sensitive core in Didier, but he's built up a thick shell around it. Whatever he's doing, he has always sought to take the lead. He is firmly convinced that he has something to offer. So he has to take charge. It's not simply to satisfy his ego or his ambition."

Instinctively, Francis Waldvogel felt this force. He counted on putting it to productive use by persuading Didier to specialize in infectious diseases. He could see a promising academic career ahead for the young doctor.

"A professor? Me? Never!" replied Didier.

"You should at least think it over."

Didier ended up following his mentor's advice.

"Now you need to do some research," suggested Waldvogel.

"Research? Me? Never!"

"Think it over."

They spoke again six months later.

"Have you thought it over?"

Didier mumbled vaguely.

"You could study the behavior of white blood cells," suggested Waldvogel.

Didier found himself in HUG's university laboratory. He knew nothing about biology and needed to learn everything, even how to use a pipette. He spent a lot of time with lab technicians. "I owe them everything," he says. He published his first scientific paper in 1985.[26]

"He was gifted, but one had the feeling that it did not interest him as much as clinical work," Waldvogel remarks. "Really, the only problem I had with Didier was because I made him do several years of research on cellular biology. He had difficulty finishing the work. Trying to prepare him for an academic career did not generate much enthusiasm in him. It was too abstract."

Didier had chosen medicine to help patients. He missed having contact with them. "I got fed up with white blood cells."

Waldvogel saw a professional crisis coming and proposed that Didier investigate nosocomial infections. It involved fieldwork in hospitals. "We had no one doing this in Geneva. We needed someone who was outstanding."

Didier seized this opportunity to escape from the laboratory. He studied infections linked to intravenous catheters. They caused 20-30% of hospital infections.[27] For example, when the needle of a catheter is inserted into a vein, it can allow the bacteria that live on the surface of the skin to be introduced into the blood. Bacteremia—the presence of bacteria in the blood—results in mortality in one out of every four cases. Thirty percent are attributable to central catheters,[28] often inserted in the jugular vein, and about one percent to peripheral catheters, often placed in the arm.

Didier readily recites these figures that were long ignored by medical professionals. "If you don't know the speed you're actually driving on a road, you can't observe the speed limits. Monitoring infections is the first step towards preventing them.[29] If the doctor doesn't have these figures, he cannot devise the right treatment strategy."

Didier paid no heed to professional taboos when he tackled the subject of nosocomial infections. In the somewhat patrician milieu of medicine, he stands out as a commoner, with the candor of an outsider. By virtue of his modest origins, he has not inherited any secret guilt or a repressed bad conscience. His work does not risk compromising any close associates. He has no family reputation to uphold, nor any vulnerabilities to protect. He started off on the path proposed by Waldvogel with the same passion he displays when he runs out onto a field for a soccer match or a skating rink for an ice hockey game. He gives the task his all, without ever thinking about his career or a winning strategy. He's the sort of man who welcomes life's surprises.

3

While carrying out numerous examinations of patients, Didier attempted to better understand the processes involved in infections. He worked day and night with the nursing staff. He learned their gestures, thought about the best method of treatment as well as the techniques that would prevent bacteria from attaching to medical devices. He adopted as his own a question first asked by Pasteur: "Instead of striving to kill microbes in wounds, wouldn't it be more reasonable not to put them there in the first place?"

Between fieldwork and the laboratory, he became an expert in the prevention of infections and the use of antibiotics. He published in scientific reviews, took part in congresses, met his peers, and visited establishments in France, Italy, Sweden, and Britain, without ever renouncing contact with the patients themselves.

As soon as a catheter needed to be withdrawn, the nurses called for Didier. He carried out the procedure, recovered the catheter, and placed it in a culture, because it was inevitably contaminated by bacteria. He separated these out by means of ultrasound or with the help of a centrifuge, identified them, and counted them. Since then, the technique has become widespread. "I simply improved on Dennis Maki's method,"[30] he says modestly.

The years went by. In 1988, Waldvogel told him: "Now we need to think about the next step in your career. In our hospital, we have no infection control program. There really aren't any in Europe. It's something you should keep in mind, you have a gift for talking to people and you're very attached to the patients. It seems to me it would be a good idea to create such a service at HUG, but first you should go to the United States."

At that time, with respect to the prevention of infections, U.S. hospitals were fifteen to twenty years ahead of Europe. From the 1970s onwards, it was increasingly common for lawyers to seek out lawsuits against hospitals in proven cases of nosocomial infections. "Dear client, if we win, you get one half, and I keep the rest. If we lose, it costs you nothing," Didier describes their shrewd tactics. Ironically though, this legal trend indirectly contributed to encouraging research on the subject.

The Centers for Disease Control and Prevention (CDC) headquartered in Atlanta, Georgia commissioned a five-year study that revealed average rates of infection of 18% in American hospitals.[31] According to the analysts, these rates could be reduced, on two conditions: 1) a doctor was appointed to take charge of prevention; and 2) the technicians in his or her service monitor infections, evaluate infection rates, and report the results to the entire hospital staff in order to raise awareness. These monitoring procedures would be accompanied by improved hygiene meaures: wearing masks and gloves, and washing hands with soap.

Didier hesitated between two hospitals, that of Dennis Maki and that of Richard Wenzel, the latter famous for having, among other things, described staphylococcus epidemics in health care centers.[32] Waldvogel's verdict left no room for doubt: "You'd be providing Maki with more than he could provide you. It's not complicated at all, go with Wenzel. You have a choice between Iowa City, Iowa City and Iowa City."

4

Iowa City nestles among cornfields to the southwest of the Great Lakes. In 1989, more than half of its 60,000 inhabitants were students. Richard Wenzel had just taken up his post at the university hospital, one of the most respected in the United States. He was given the mission of making it the leader in the field of prevention. He started by multiplying the equivalent of road radars. Each time an infection was detected, his technicians analyzed its nature and origin.

Regularly, they released statistics on infection rates. The initial figures were not at all reassuring: nosocomial infections affected on average 18% of patients. Without serious consequences in the majority of cases, they entailed extra days of hospitalization, which multiplied costs by five. A bacteremia cost on average 40,000 dollars.[33] So prevention was doubly advantageous. By saving lives, one could save money, a consideration that would please hospital directors, often better accountants than doctors.

Wenzel's preventive work brought about a reduction in infection rates by a third, from 18% to 12%. But in U.S. hospitals, which did not have any prevention program, the rates increased, to almost 21%. "Medicine is changing," comments Didier. "It's becoming more and more invasive. And only the patients most at risk remain in hospital. That explains the increase in rates where nothing has been done to fight against infections. The difference between hospitals with and without prevention programs is almost 50%," he groans. "In the first group, you're twice as unlikely to become ill, twice as unlikely to die."

While becoming specialized in epidemiology—a discipline not taught in Geneva—Didier made the rounds of the hospital departments with Wenzel's technicians. "I did not understand how it worked. We didn't have these kinds of experts. I learned everything from them." At the same time, he examined patients and taught courses on infectious diseases, without neglecting to write more scientific papers.

This intense activity left him little free time, but when the opportunity presented itself, Didier and Brigitte took their children to the shore of the lake formed by the Iowa River, for water-skiing, canoeing, swimming and picnics. In this region far from the great urban centers, life passed by quietly. "He never attached much importance to relaxation," Brigitte amends this impression. "For him, we weren't there to enjoy ourselves or to rest, but to serve. He's always been hyperactive."

Back at the hospital, one thing struck Didier very quickly. Wenzel's technicians had barely any medical qualifications. They were allowed to look at patients' files, but they didn't interact with the doctors. They limited themselves to recording infections and calculating the rates. Didier found this passiveness incomprehensible. He'd already practiced internal medicine in Geneva. He'd worked with cardiologists, pneumologists and nephrologists. In Canada, during his fourth year of study, he had the chance to assist surgeons. When seeing patients, he made it a habit to perform a hands-on examination. In his eyes, limiting oneself to stoically measuring excessive infection rates was not the right method.

Unlike climatologists who helplessly register the warming of the biosphere, Didier wanted to act. Upon his return to Switzerland, he would not hire technicians with minimal medical training, but instead highly qualified nurses. They would observe, then intervene, and they would be given the means to do so. In 1991, during a trip to Geneva, he outlined his action plan to HUG's head nurse, Nicole Fichter, who was delighted by it. "I'd visited him in the United States. I too was convinced he would need clinical nurse specialists."

In collaboration with Nicole, Didier then took the most important decision of his life. Having been a doctor up until this point, he would become a sociologist. He would henceforth take an interest in the behavior of health care workers, and not just catheters.

In the spring of 1992, Nicole Fichter sent four clinical nurse specialists to Iowa City to train with Wenzel's teams. Upon their return to Geneva, they found themselves left to their own devices. "While waiting for Didier to join us," recalls Josiane Sztajzel-Boissard, "we only had one assignment: writing a report. It was at that point that the MRSA epidemic broke out. We knew methicillin-resistant *Staphylococcus aureus* existed, but it was another thing entirely to discover it in our own hospital. We tried putting in place a training and prevention program. Isolating patients, hand hygiene, attacking the staphylococci with a cocktail of antibiotics. We went round all the services. Everyone listened to us, as there was a bit of a panic at the time."

When Didier returned to Switzerland for good in October 1992, no one doubted any longer the need to set up a new infection control and prevention service. "The battle against MRSA meant that everyone knew us," explains Josiane. Along with her and her three nursing colleagues, Pascale Herrault, Nicole Henry and Anna Alexiou, Didier decided to measure the hospital's infection rates. Some conservative service chiefs who were jealous of their prerogatives did not look kindly on this study. They disliked the idea of an audit. "Why does he have four nurse specialists? They'd be more useful working in emergency." At the same time, HUG's administrative direction became involved. It was interested in nosocomial infections and wanted to place Didier under its wing. Waldvogel, on the other hand, sought to keep him in the academic domain. "There were tensions," he observes, "some exchanges back and forth that weren't always handled well."

For Didier, there was never a question of giving up. He and his team trained, tested its methods, and perfected them. "I joined them at that point," recounts Valérie Sauvan. "I replaced Josiane who was about to have a baby. The others looked at me a little dismissively at first. I was quite young. We spent a week going through all the services, seeing all the patients, recording all the infections. We were fanatical about it. We completed our normal working hours, and then worked on the study from 8 p.m. to 1 a.m. Didier bought us chocolate. It was so funny. This young doctor made me want to get fully involved. We had the feeling that things were moving in the right direction, so we followed him."

Very quickly, the figures emerged: 18% of infections on average, with peaks of over 30% in intensive care. Didier refused to believe it at first. "We are in Switzerland, not Zimbabwe, after all." Three months later, once the data had been digested, they repeated the study: 17%. Another three months went by and they once again obtained 18%.[34] The nurses worked ceaselessly. Didier followed up on their work, checking their results. And they followed up on him, checking his findings. They compared data. The rates remained worrying. "And elsewhere?" Didier wondered anxiously, aware that his hospital was one of the best in the country.

The infections spared no service. They circulated throughout the hospital, and no barrier could stop them. Didier searched for a prime cause. One day in 1994, a nurse spoke to him about a patient infected by a resistant germ. The following day, the same germ was found in a neighboring room. "Something transferred it!" Little by little, the truth became obvious. "We have infections in our establishment," reasoned Didier. "We know they're conveyed by the ventilation system, the instruments, and the patients themselves, but above all by the hands of health care workers. We must not have been careful enough in that respect."

And so the story of Ignaz Semmelweis began to haunt him.

CHAPTER II

THE SPIRITUAL HEIR OF IGNAZ SEMMELWEIS

1

The girl screams: they should let her give birth right there on the damp pavement. She does not want to be taken to the general hospital, but this child-mother has nowhere else to go. Some men lay her out in a cart. She desperately throws herself against them with her last bit of strength. Assuming she's being irrational, they tie her down in order to carry her through the streets. She thinks she is doomed. Like all other paupers in Vienna, Austria of 1847, she knows that in the hospital's maternity ward, one woman out of three dies of puerperal fever—a cervical infection contracted in the time just following childbirth.

A young doctor with an egg-shaped skull leans over her bedside. He holds out his hands. "I won't poison you," he promises in a strong Hungarian accent. It's difficult to take him seriously. People often make fun of him. The young woman doesn't have the energy for that. Her clothes are removed. He gently examines her. She trembles while he spreads his fingers in order to estimate the dilation of her cervix. He reassures her. The baby is in the right position. She looks around with frightened eyes. There are ten other women present, all of them just as miserable, all just as worried. A twelfth arrives, screaming. The doctor hurries over to her. The doctor examines her, grimaces, and isolates her. "She has the fever," the women whisper fearfully. He shakes his head, returns to them, and goes from one on to the next, measuring cervical dilation. In the days that follow, eleven out of the twelve will be dead corpses.

Ignaz Semmelweis was stricken with remorse by this incident. He had never been able to bear the death of his patients and now he had definite proof that he was a murderer. This certainty would compel him ten years later to publish an implacable pamphlet aimed at obstetricians: "Against them I stand as a resolute adversary, just as one must stand against the parties to a crime! For my part, I can only regard them as assassins. [...] It is not the birthing houses that need to be closed in order to put a stop to the disasters one abhors, but the obstetricians who need to be removed from them, for it is they who act as veritable epidemics."[35]

In those dark years, puerperal fever, not yet regarded as a nosocomial infection, was rife.[36] "It kills, whenever it likes: in Vienna, 28% in November, 40% in January. Its reach extends, right around the world," wrote Louis-Ferdinand Céline in his medical thesis of 1924.[37] It almost sounds as if he was already preparing the chopped-up prose style he used in his famous novel, *Journey to the End of the Night*. "Death leads the dance... with bells around them... Dubois in Paris reports... 18 %... Schuld in Berlin 26 %... Simpson 22 %... in Turin out of one hundred giving birth, thirty-two die."

These figures are similar to the infection rates observed by Didier Pittet, but in 19th century Vienna, as in other European cities, they referred to mortality, not infections. In statistical terms, we have certainly retreated from that level of horror. Nevertheless, the number of present day deaths remains unacceptable.

Didier Pittet cannot tolerate them any more today then Ignaz Semmelweis could then. Separated by one hundred and fifty years, they follow parallel trajectories.

2

Didier likes to retell the story of Semmelweis's child-hood. He was born in Buda on the Danube's west bank, before the city was attached to Pest and became the capital of Hungary. He speaks of Semmelweis's father, a prosperous grocer who wanted his son to become a jurist. Didier must be thinking of his own father, Robert, who was an artisan. So we have two sons of rather modest origins whose parents pushed them towards higher education.

Ignaz left Hungary to complete his law degree in Vienna. However, he turned away from that profession to take up medicine. His professor, named Skoda, took him under his wing. But Skoda seems to fear his student's budding genius and preferred to steer him towards obstetrics in order not to be overshadowed. In contrast, Francis Waldvogel supported Didier Pittet. He encouraged Didier to develop his talent. These two lives that began with great similarity begin to experience significant differences. The main cause of their divergence, however, is already quite obvious. "Semmelweis was all fire," wrote Louis-Ferdinand Céline. But Didier burns with a more enchanting flame. All of his nurses speak to me of him with knowing smiles, describing his powerful charisma.

Faced with the ravages of puerperal fever, Ignaz was at as much of a loss as Didier when confronted by nosocomial infections. So he observed, measured, reported his findings, and made a fundamental discovery. At the general hospital in Vienna, two maternity clinics were located side by side. In the clinic run by Professor Klein in which medical students attended births, mortality was higher than in the clinic overseen by Professor Bartsch, where midwives were in attendance: 9% compared to 3% over the period between 1841 and 1846. And these averages were almost reassuring because they smoothed over some truly horrific peaks.

The difference could not be attributed to the patients themselves. Equally impoverished and abandoned, they were sent to one clinic or the other on alternate days. Nor could one suspect that some mysterious pollutant in the air halted as if by magic at the door to Bartsch's clinic. "The cosmic, terrestrial, or atmospheric causes invoked in connection with puerperal fever have no basis in fact since one dies more often in Klein's clinic than in Bartsch's, and more often in a hospital than in the city at large, where the cosmic, terrestrial or whatever conditions you like are quite the same."[38] "The cause I am seeking is in our clinic and nowhere else," Semmelweis deduced.

It did not take him long to deduce that the medical students played a key role in the tragedy. As a test, Semmelweis sent them to attend births in Bartsch's clinic, and observed the mortality rates reversed. He had no explanation, but at least he found the guilty parties. He asked them why they had not questioned the reasons for the death of certain patients when others survived. Concerning the work in Professor Klein's clinic, he wrote: "All that is done here seems quite futile to me, the deaths simply go on, one after another." Semmelweis's relationship deteriorated with Klein, as the latter seemed completely indifferent to the carnage for which he was responsible.

Semmelweis traveled to Venice during a leave from the hospital. Upon his return, he learned that one of his friends died. Jakob Kolletschka was an anatomy professor, who was wounded during an autopsy by a student and died several days later with symptoms of puerperal fever. However, his death was not entirely in vain. Everything lit up with a macabre glow. "It is the fingers of students, soiled while performing dissections, which carry the fatal cadaveric particles to the genital organs of pregnant women and in particular to the region of the cervix," Semmelweis concluded. If Bartsch's clinic was less affected by puerperal fever, it was because the midwives there did not perform autopsies.

That same night, Semmelweis roamed the hospital, looking for the most corrosive and foul-smelling product used by the cleaning staff. He found chlorinated lime solution, whose disinfecting properties had been demonstrated by a French pharmacist in 1822. The following day, he demanded that the entire staff rub their hands with this vile mixture for five minutes before leaving the autopsy room. It was veritable torture. The solution caused stinging in the eyes and irritated skin to the point of bleeding. But the results were there for all to see: mortality rates plummeted.

Then came that fateful day in October 1847 when Semmelweis lost eleven women following successive vaginal examinations. He deduced from this tragedy that disease particles could also be transferred between living persons. "The hands, by simple contact, can be infectious."[39] He then imposed a protocol of hand hygiene with chlorinated lime between examinations of each patient. The mortality rate fell to 0.23%. It was a prodigious success. One of the greatest medical feats of all time. Yet Semmelweis was dismissed from the hospital.

3

In 1994, Didier understood that neglect of hand hygiene was in large part the cause of the infections observed at HUG, he could not help recall the tragedy that befell Semmelweis. He drew lessons from the failures of his predecessor, and there were many.

Semmelweis behaved like a tyrant, often violently. A poor psychologist, he imposed his remedy and permitted no discussion. He ignored the chlorinated lime's awful smell, the irritations, and the inevitable cases of dermatitis. The immediate consequence was that the students complained of "unhealthy hand washing", and soon they were boycotting it altogether. To Semmelweis, this was sheer stupidity in the face of the cruel mortality figures, and thus intolerable.

According to Louis-Ferdinand Céline, the medical students went so far as to deliberately contaminate patients, in an attempt to discredit Semmelweis's methods. Semmelweis entrusted his friends with the task of stepping forward in his defense. But errors slipped into their speeches on his behalf, which were ultimately used to denounce him. Cursed with a combination of excessive enthusiasm, intolerance, and pride, he made no effort to be pleasant to anyone. He chose to stand alone against all adversity, to see himself as some sort of heroic knight.

Semmelweis wrote in a letter: "Destiny has chosen me to be the missionary of truth with respect to the measures one must take to avoid and combat the puerperal scourge. I have long since ceased to reply to the attacks I am constantly subjected to; the order of things must prove to my opponents that I am entirely right without it being necessary for me to participate in polemics that can now in no way serve the progress of truth."[40]

In his medical thesis, Louis-Ferdinand Céline offers a scathing verdict: "As for Semmelweis, it seems that his discovery outstripped the powers of his genius." The Hungarian clung to an ideal conception of the truth. He forgot that, once applied, hand hygiene could save the lives of millions of women. He gave up his combat on the grounds that he was right and that fighting to win people over would demean him. He did not take the trouble to listen. He heaped insults upon his adversaries. He was clumsy, boorish, a man too driven to consider of the happiness of his contemporaries. He neglected his few friends, and then he left them suddenly.

Returning to the city of his birth, he ended up securing a post in another maternity clinic. There, he wrote his great work in which he exhaustively elaborated his theory, supported by dozens of statistical tables. He discovered that the epidemic of puerperal fever began in the 1820s, when the practice of autopsies first became widespread. Soon promoted head of the clinic, he again imposed a hand hygiene protocol and repeated his spectacular results. But he was once more dismissed, too insensitive to the needs and desires of those around him to persuade them change their behavior. He did not know how to lead them without resorting to the whip. Wounded, embittered, he walked the streets of Buda and of Pest, putting up posters warning husbands not to place their wives in the hands of obstetricians. "Anyone who enters a maternity ward without washing their hands is a criminal," he proclaimed.

This brilliant innovator would soon sink into madness, a degeneration that was accelerated by syphilis. He died at the age of 47, before Pasteur founded the science of microbiology. Forty years after his disappearance, his reputation would be restored. Louis-Ferdinand Céline wrote in his thesis: "He showed us the dangers of wanting too much good for men. It's an age-old lesson that is always renewed. Suppose that today, in a similar fashion, another naïve person comes along to cure cancer. He has no idea what kind of tune he'll be forced right away to dance to! It would be truly phenomenal! Oh, he'd need to be careful! Oh, he'd better be forewarned! He'd really have to watch his step!"

Didier read this warning when he plunged into Semmelweis's work. An obvious truth stared him in the face: one cannot do good for others, and still less for the community as a whole, against their will. Before proposing a plan of action, Didier would need to observe health care workers constantly. He would not be listened to unless he studied their every gesture. A whole set of human factors needed to be integrated into the plan. Being right too soon would serve no purpose.

4

In 1994, Didier studied the entire body of scientific literature on hand hygiene. There were several studies of the efficacy of antiseptic soap,[41] but since Semmelweis, the existing state of affairs was often simply accepted. Medical personnel knew they should wash their hands, but no one attached much importance to the practice. Doctors preferred to take an interest in more technical matters, leaving the whole question of hand hygiene to the nurses. Didier did indeed discuss the issue with his four nurses. "You know, Didier, hand hygiene… it's surely our daily bread, but it's difficult."

"Why is it difficult?"

"Because there's a whole treatment procedure."

"And what if we did a real study of it?"

Another boss would simply have ordered a study. Didier asked his nurses if they agreed with the idea. He involved them in every decision, just like a good manager with a degree from a business school. One could not accuse him of being manipulative. "It's his boy scout side," says Valérie Sauvan. "He carries everyone along with him." For good reason, since he had in fact been a boy scout, a captain of his soccer and hockey teams, summer camp counselor, and he organized all the parties during medical school. He feels at ease in the community. "But he's always two steps ahead of us," points out Sylvie Touveneau, another nurse who soon joined the initial team.

Didier had already formulated his question: What makes people wash their hands or not? "We need to do a study of the risk factors," he concluded. Along with Sylvie, Valérie, and their three colleagues, Nicole, Pascale, and Anna, he devised an observation protocol. In December, day and night, on weekends as well as during the week, his team systematically visited all the services at HUG. During twenty-minute periods, the nurses noted whether the medical personnel washed their hands every time a hand hygiene opportunity presented itself, such as manipulating a catheter.

"Didier, it's appalling," cried Sylvie Touveneau upon returning from intensive care. "I was working there myself three weeks ago and I forgot to wash, just like everybody else. I can't believe it." By becoming an observer, she was made aware of her own shortcomings and they alarmed her. The first results came back.[42] The average compliance rate was 48%. For nurses it was 52%; doctors 30%; midwives 66%. The latter were perhaps influenced by Semmelweis's story. Radiology technicians, only 8%. "That's catastrophic," moaned Didier.

"Do you think anyone ever explained it to them?" a nurse wondered.

She went to find the technicians in question and discovered that no one had ever told them they should wash their hands.

The figures from the study were revealing. Lack of time led to poor compliance with hand hygiene. Overall, the more occasions for washing hands arose—such as in the emergency room—the less staff actually washed.

Didier presented the results to his nurses. They smiled at him.

"We already knew that."

"What? You knew that?"

"Well, yes. When we're stressed, when there's too much work, we don't always make time to wash our hands."

Didier was stunned. He had set up a rigorous epidemiological study only to end up with an obvious result. The instructions all stipulated that one should go to the sink, turn on the water, lather one's hands with soap, rub them together, rinse them and dry them. No one had ever asked if it were possible in practical terms. "To the point that all the medical staff firmly claimed they washed their hands 80% of the time, when this was far from the truth."

At the beginning of 1995, Didier visited the intensive care unit with a stopwatch in his hand. He discovered that nurses had on average 22 occasions to wash their hands per hour. In order to wash thoroughly, they needed one to two minutes. "When you multiply that by 22, it's impossible. You can't clean your hands using soap and water. It takes too long." But there was another remedy available. "We should use alcohol. No need to go to the sink every time. We put it on our hands. When it's dry, they're clean."

This idea was incredibly simple. Everyone knows that alcohol is a powerful antiseptic. Every child cries when they feel its sting in their cuts and scratches. "But it was not used frequently in hospitals," Didier recalls. "We consumed 15,000 bottles per year back then, as opposed to 250,000 today! It was something reserved almost exclusively for use in the laboratory."

That is where Didier had an extraordinary stroke of luck. "William Griffiths, the pharmacist at HUG, was an expert on alcohol-based solutions."

This Englishman, wearing his hair tied back in a ponytail, received a degree in Pharmacology from the University of Liverpool in 1964 before moving to Switzerland because the salaries were higher, or perhaps it was just out of love for the beautiful scenery, which stimulated his photographer's eye. He settled in Fribourg and worked in the cantonal hospital.

In 1974, the hospital administration officially asked him to create an alcohol-based rinse for hands. An article just published in the *British Medical Journal* explained how rubbing one's hands with 10 ml of alcohol mixed with chlorhexidine—a powerful antiseptic patented in 1954—reduced bacterial accumulation on hands much more effectively than traditional techniques using antiseptic soap.[43] "But the only product available on the market back then was expensive and inadequate," explains William. His passion for finding the most elegant chemical formula, his hyper-sensitivity, as well as a perfectionism that verged on idealism, led him to concoct 50 variations, each of whose antiseptic power and stability he then tested relentlessly.

In mid-1976, William proposed a disinfectant formulation derived from the one presented in the *British Medical Journal*: 75 % isopropanol, a synthetic alcohol selected for its immediate action upon bacteria; 0.5 % chlorhexidine to prevent the bacteria from attaching themselves subsequently and lingering, which was particularly useful to surgeons. He added water to these two essential ingredients because a 100% alcohol-based rinse failed to destroy germs. This detail is not devoid of philosophical interest: more is not necessarily better.

At Fribourg, the hospital did not have the budget needed to patent the formula. So it was offered freely to other Swiss hospitals. At the request of HUG's head pharmacist, it was sent to Geneva in 1978, soon followed by William in person. Since then, he continued to experiment with the formulation, adding emulsifiers to render the rinse less aggressive for hands. "William was already prepared," recounts Didier. "As if he'd been waiting all this time for me to come and find him. He's the father of the alcohol-based handrub."

In 1995, they tested the formula with the nurses. "William still had fifty thousand ideas about variations. He hesitated, going back to previous attempts. I was finally obliged to choose, otherwise we'd still be experimenting." Didier's pragmatism complemented the pharmacist's artistic sense. Gradually, it became obvious that the alcohol-based rinse was in fact better for cleansing hands. The dermatologists explained that soap is the skin's worst enemy. It breaks the disulfide bridges in the proteins linking the skin's cells.[44] The skin then allows the water it contains to escape. As it dries, it loses its tonicity.[45]

Alcohol appeared to be the miracle product. Everyone had it right under their noses, everyone knew its antiseptic value, but no one had thought of distributing it widely for use within hospitals. "For a long time, that had been my dream," William relates. "But Didier made it possible by observing that it was unfeasible to use soap for every hand hygiene opportunity."

In the spring of 1996, John Boyce stopped off in Geneva after attending a congress on staphylococcus in nearby Annecy, France. "He was a friend from way back," Didier says. "We'd been running into one another since I started out. He's one of the best experts on infectious diseases in the United States. He's also concerned with hand hygiene and works with Elaine Larson, the leading American specialist in the field." Didier communicated the first results to him. They showed that compliance improved with the switch to alcohol and infections diminished. Then he sent Boyce to visit HUG with Valérie Sauvan. She presented to him the five key moments when, according to the first studies, hand cleansing was required.[46]

1) Before touching a patient.

2) Before any aseptic procedure (taking a blood sample, for example).

3) After any risk of exposure to a biological fluid.

4) After touching a patient.

5) After having been in contact with a patient's environment.

"I don't know quite how to describe it," Didier says. "John Boyce had something of a revelation. He went back to the United States with some bottles of our rinse and started to test it in his own hospital. He was the first to believe in the idea outside of HUG."

A few months later, the CDC in Atlanta asked Boyce to revise the official U.S. recommendations on hand hygiene, whose previous edition dated back to 1985. "Didier, you should write these with me. We can't do it without you." The objective was to define when and how hands needed to be cleansed, justifying each choice with scientific studies. "It was an enormous task," explains Didier. "We read 1,500 articles; I had them piled up all over my living room." He smiles. "They paid us the royal sum of 2,000 dollars for our trouble."

Didier is amused by this anecdote, which shows how surreal investment priorities in medicine can be. A handful of dollars was spent to write up the recommendations[47] that, once they were applied, would save thousands of lives every day. If the pharmaceutical companies had found a way to make big profits from this, money would have flowed freely, even if the actual health impact were far less great.

In order to convince the medical profession of the pertinence of the new recommendations, John Boyce made use of a month's worth of examinations of patients with infectious diseases to carry out a radical experiment. During the first two weeks, at every hand hygiene opportunity, he washed his hands with soap. As a result, his hands were covered with abrasions and red patches, as if they spent five minutes in Semmelweis's chlorinated lime solution. The following two weeks, Boyce used HUG's alcohol-based rinse. In just a few days, his hands healed, regaining their suppleness and their normal color.[48] "We had proof by absurdity that alcohol was the only viable option if one wanted to increase compliance with hand hygiene."

CHAPTER III

RESISTANCE TO CHANGE

The Palais des Congrès conference center in the southwestern French town of Arcachon, 8th Congress of the French Society of Hospital Hygiene June 1997, exactly one hundred and fifty years after Semmelweis's groundbreaking discovery. Loud booing resounds in the auditorium. "We're going to drink your alcohol!" the doctors are yelling at Sylvie Touveneau, who is number five in Didier's team. A serious-looking woman from the Poitou region of France and highly capable at her job, curses them silently. They have no respect at all for a mere nurse, and no doubt would have behaved better if her boss had come to speak instead. The bastards are amusing themselves at her expense. *A lowly worker such as myself has no business telling you what to do in your hospitals, is that it?*

But she had been rigorous in her arguments. She presented all the studies carried out by HUG.[49] The measurements of infection rates, and then those concerning hand hygiene compliance. She showed that soap did not work, as opposed to alcohol. *They can't argue with the figures. They're irrefutable.* Dismayed, on the verge of panic, and disgusted, she looks once more upon hundreds of hostile faces before finally leaving the podium, furious. The doctors gathered here in the year 1997 have reacted exactly like Semmelweis's detractors. Through fear of the unknown, special interests clash with the general good.

"I know positively [...] that each of us has the plague within him; no one, no one on earth is free from it," wrote Albert Camus in *The Plague*. "And I know, too, that we must keep endless watch on ourselves lest in a careless moment we breathe in someone's face and fasten the infection upon him. What's natural is the microbe. All the rest—health, integrity, purity (if you like)—is a product of the human will, of a vigilance that must never falter. The good man, the man who infects hardly anyone, is the man who has the fewest lapses of attention. And it needs tremendous will-power, a never ending tension of the mind to avoid such lapses."[50]

Didier is not angry with anyone, and especially not those lacking willpower. He understands them. Contrary to Semmelweis, he operates in the context of an economy of peace. Hand hygiene is not something that can be imposed by force. It would be dangerous to believe that thousands of tragic deaths could be avoided simply by decree. In practice, the straight line is not the shortest path. Water, when it runs, sometimes wavers. Even on an apparently flat windshield, droplets move around invisible obstacles. Nevertheless, it always ends up running to the bottom. Everyone should be allowed to adopt their own pace, as long as the destination is reached.

Didier did not impose change, but rather he offered the possibility of making alcohol available to everyone working in the hospital environment, explaining the benefits and releasing the results of his studies every six months. In the first three years, the use of alcohol at HUG multiplied by five, and infection rates were halved. "It's working," Didier observed with satisfaction. He no longer had any doubts, but the most difficult task still lay ahead: persuading the rest of the world.

2

In order for alcohol to be used consistently, it needed to be placed right at the point of patient care. A nurse who biked had the idea of using two metal bicycle clips arranged head to tail. The first would be clipped onto hospital bed railings, while the other held the bottles of alcohol. The team of night custodians assembled 5,000 of these pairs of clips that were soon distributed through all of HUG's services. One morning, Didier passed by in front of the emergency waiting room. The door was slightly open and he could see dozens of clips stapled to the ceiling inside. The revolt had begun. The pretext invoked was that nurses kept tearing their stockings on the clips, and sometimes they were even injured by them.

It is more difficult to support change than to oppose it. Didier watched this struggle play out, almost stoically. He understood that caution is a socially healthy reaction. This defense mechanism invented by evolution is easily illustrated by the metaphor of the crazy toads.[51] Every year during the month of March, toads return to the pond of their birth to reproduce. If the pond has subsequently dried-up or been polluted, the toads die. If all toads behaved in this fashion, the slightest hazard would put the entire species at risk. Luckily, about 10% of toads, called "crazy" because they behave differently from the others, venture elsewhere each spring. When they discover new ponds, they will copulate with other toads they find there, contributing their genes and participating in the renewal and propagation of their species. But if all toads were crazy, or followed the lead of a crazy individual, this would also place the survival of the species in jeopardy. Most of them would perish along the way, never finding a welcoming pond.

And the moral of this story? Most individuals stick to the routine that works for them, while a few pioneers experiment and head out into the unknown. If they discover benefits, others will follow. If not, the majority remains safely behind, avoiding general annihilation. Consequently, the innovator must accept resistance. It is a necessary ordeal. All worthwhile ideas must be capable of eventually surmounting this kind of survival test.

The head of the maintenance service at HUG entered the stage. "Monsieur Pittet, this won't do at all. Your rinse is staining the floors." Didier had to persuade him to try to find some kind of alcohol-resistant coating for the linoleum floors. At the same time, Didier suggested to William Griffiths that he come up with a new gel formulation. "There would be less spillage." The Faculty of Pharmacy in Geneva examined the problem. Gradually, it turned into an interdisciplinary project, with all of the hospital's craft professions engaging in this experiment.

The nurses started grumbling again. At their request, the bike clips were removed and replaced by portable bottles. These created unsightly bulges in their uniform pockets so William Griffiths replaced them with flat flasks that were much more discreet. Moral objections were raised in the neonatal unit, due to an apprehension about touching premature babies with hands imbibed with alcohol. There were unfounded fears that babies' skin would not tolerate it. Above all, there was a taboo of mixing purity and impurity, alcohol being better known for sending people to hospital than for preventing them from being infected while they were there.

Compliance with hand hygiene was weak in that unit, 34%, even though newborns were among those most at risk.[52] "That's true for all the extremes of life," comments Sylvie Touveneau. "The very young, the very old, the very ill." The clips on the emergency room ceiling, the fear of alcohol in the neonatal nursery, were signs that resistance was strongest where a change in habits was truly needed. The system defended itself energetically in its most sensitive regions. It resembled a living being that did not want to die.

There were reasons to be optimistic. In the neonatal nursery, a study conducted by Didier and his team revealed that hand hygiene compliance improved in the critical phases.[53] So health care workers were altering their habits. This shift was their own rebellion in a way. Once they were warned of the risks and trained, the change accelerated. In extreme conditions, such as an emergency room or an intensive care unit, change has to emerge from the individuals involved. It takes root, grows new shoots, and eventually becomes a forest. Reforms imposed from above don't work. They crash straight into a system that remains camped on its existing position. We should retain this lesson when it comes to other domains. People are not ready to change their behavior until they've been exposed to danger.

3

Resistance from medical practitioners was followed by an editorial struggle. A fundamental discovery hardly makes an impact unless it is presented in a reputable review. In 1995, after having presented a summary of his work at a medical congress in Lyon, France,[54] Didier took a gamble. Without any recommendation, he submitted the study on hand hygiene compliance that had been carried out the previous year to the prestigious U.S. monthly review, *Annals of Internal Medicine*. A few weeks later, the editors wrote back expressing their interest. "But the editors asked us to revise our mathematical model of statistical analysis, then answer a series of questions, then furnish new results, and then they asked us to shorten the text. We wasted four years on this business. For them, it wasn't urgent. Everyone knew that people weren't washing their hands." The article was finally published in January 1999.[55]

The medical community discovered that out of 2,843 opportunities for hand washing, compliance was 48% on average, with the lowest rate in intensive care, at 36%. "Even though observational data cannot prove causality, the association between noncompliance and intensity of care suggests that understaffing may decrease quality of patient care." A graph showed that as the number of opportunities increased, the rate of compliance declined. The article concluded with a brief analysis of the five critical moments for hand hygiene.

The very same day the article was published, Don Goldman, a friend who taught at Harvard Medical School, called Didier: "Your paper is essential reading. It's proof that alcohol should be introduced." Didier explained to him that he had started these experiments back in 1995. At the same time, he realized that if he'd published sooner, he would not have had time to develop his program calmly. Other hospitals would have entered into competition with HUG.

Didier submitted two new articles to *The Lancet*, the leading review of medical science since 1823. As renown tends to attract further renown, the editors accepted both articles. The first was published in May 2000 and dealt with infections by catheter.[56] The second appeared in October 2000 and described hand hygiene procedures using the alcohol-based handrub, soon known as the "Geneva Model" of hand hygiene.[57] It was a consecration.

Between 1994 and 1997, 20,000 opportunities for practicing hand hygiene were studied. When the alcohol-based handrub was made available, the rate of compliance rose from 48% to 67%, and average infection rates fell from 16.9% to 9.9 %. The transmission of multiresistant staphylococci decreased from 2.16 to 0.93 episodes per 1,000 days of hospitalization. All of the lights turned green as the use of alcohol increased. A more diligent practice of hand hygiene meant less infection, less suffering, and fewer deaths.

"Didier, it's incredible," the dean of the University of Geneva exclaimed in delight. "I've seen your papers in *The Lancet*. I didn't know you could get published in such a high-level journal!"

"You were the one who appointed me professor."

"Yes, but to climb so high with your hand cleansing thing!"

The fate of an idea depends greatly on the convergence of circumstances. In the case of the Geneva Model, one could not attribute its success to a mere publishing breakthrough. Since 1996, John Boyce had been using alcohol in his hospital. In 1998, Jonathan Cohen, the head of the microbiology department at Imperial College in London, asked Didier to help set up an infection prevention program at Hammersmith Hospital. "It was an immense honor," comments Didier. "This was the place with the most winners of the Nobel Prize in Medicine." He was even offered a post there. Didier accepted, but then turned it down because Brigitte and his four children were not ready to follow him to London. "We went through a tremendous crisis." But he was still looking straight ahead, almost blindly.

4

After the publication in *The Lancet* in October 2000, no one could ignore the virtues of the alcohol-based handrub. Practitioners came to visit HUG from all over the world; from Australia, the United States, Belgium. Doctors left with bottles of handrub in order to establish the Geneva Model in their own hospitals.

The affair soon took on an unexpected geopolitical twist. At the beginning of 2001, Didier received a call from the National Patient Safety Agency (NPSA) in the UK: "Could we come see your program?" Didier invited them to Geneva. Five of them came, studied everything for a week, and then announced their intention to launch a national campaign in Britain. "Would you care to help us?" The idea of refusing did not even occur to Didier.

Britain became the first country to promote hand hygiene with alcohol-based handrubs in all its hospitals. And it worked. It provided proof that the results achieved in Geneva could be reproduced elsewhere, and on a wider scale. Didier was relieved. Some skeptics had postulated the existence of a "Pittet effect", attributing HUG's extraordinary success to Didier's presence, and to his personal charisma. It was nothing of the sort. The method was universal, and its proliferation had some surprising consequences.

One British nurse of Islamic background had a problem when her father objected to her use of alcohol to disinfect her hands. "We don't know what to do," said the NPSA. "We have many Muslim health care workers." Didier was dumbfounded. For a moment, he feared a *fatwa*. He consulted a doctor friend in Saudi Arabia and they decided to put together a working group with members of the Islamic clergy. They met in Geneva, then in Riyadh, reviewing everything in the Quran that concerned alcohol. At the end of four months, a verdict was reached. Muslims are of course forbidden to drink alcohol, or ingest it by any other means. The Quran is inflexible on this.

Worried, Didier called up Lindsay Grayson, an Australian friend who was evaluating various alcohol-based handrubs. "Can you find out if skin absorbs alcohol? You'll need to test different alcohols." There exist two general types: ethyl alcohol (or ethanol) and isopropyl alcohol (or isopropanol). Lindsay had test subjects disinfect their hands thirty times per hour, with blood tests before and after. He also went to the police, borrowed their breathalyzer, and got his subjects to blow into it. At the end, he published a paper with the amusing title: "Can alcohol-based hand-rub solutions cause you to lose your driver's license?"[58]

No, of course not. With ethanol, only a few molecules passed into the blood and the lungs, about as much as when one drinks a liter of orange juice. And isopropanol does not cross the skin barrier at all. "It was a relief," Didier admits. "It would have been terrible if we could not use the solution everywhere." The Muslim World League met. It proclaimed that the formulation based on isopropanol was compatible with the Quran.[59] "Today, there's a high degree of acceptance in many Islamic countries. They're now consuming large quantities of alcohol. And in principle, they're not drinking it,' Didier says with a laugh.

However, the comment is not entirely absurd. At HUG, the use of alcohol increased in a linear fashion over the years. And similar trends was observed in Britain and other countries that adopted the Geneva Model. In Russia, on the other hand, there was an exponential progression of alcohol intake after only three months. "They're drinking the solution," Didier guffaws. So now, in Russia, the pharmacists add propanone, a chemical that causes people to vomit.

"That's incredible," Didier continues saying in amazement. He himself cannot stand the taste of alcohol except when mixed into a recipe. He has never been a drinker. "At the beginning, you have to force yourself," his friends explained to him when he was a teenager. But he never gave into peer pressure. He always remained himself, resolute. He defends hand hygiene with the same rigor. Nothing can divert him from the path he has chosen for himself.

Since childhood, he has followed a sort of cult of hygiene, involving a fondness for sports, a balanced diet, and the rejection of tobacco. It's a far cry from any kind of austere Gandhi-like regimen, but he naturally applies the same principles of moderation to his life that account for his scientific choices.

Without his strong personal integrity, he would not have resisted pressure from the pharmaceutical companies. "I was spending my time assessing their products; I couldn't be pals with them." Before the British campaign was launched, he worried about the quality of the alcohol-based rinses and gels available in the UK. "There's no point putting them in your hospitals if they don't work." There was a lot at stake. He couldn't risk failure over such a stupid detail. He sent the ten gels and the four rinses available to three laboratories to evaluate their effectiveness. The verdict was incontrovertible: although the rinses were suitable, none of the gels had sufficient antiseptic power. "The tested hand gels should be considered a retrograde step for hand hygiene," Didier contended in a new article published in *The Lancet* in April 2002.[60]

In the days that followed, three CEOs from the incriminated pharmaceutical companies arranged for appointments with him. Two were Americans and one was British. Wearing red ties and blue shirts, complete with briefcases, they arrived in his office and all of them said the same thing: "Your tests are false."

"Listen, we used three different labs, with world experts..."

"We don't agree with you."

Didier quickly discovered that the three companies in question knew perfectly well that their products were unsuitable, but wanted to run down their existing stocks before they launched a new generation of gels on the market. "I haven't always made friends. Those people hated me." All the more so because, like most experts of infectious diseases, Didier is fighting against the abuse of antibiotics. "Because we pick up the resistant germs in our hospital services. One day, we're going to have a serious health problem as a result." For now, Didier is in conflict with the pharmaceutical corporations. His conscience stands opposed to them.

Summer of 1994, at a hospital in California.[61] Out of 55 patients who underwent cardiovascular surgery, seven were contaminated by bacteria known to cause urinary infections and pneumonia. One of the patients died. After DNA analysis, the investigators were unable to identify any strain of the identified bacteria within the hospital or on the hands of health care workers. The investigation was suspended, having turned up a single clue: the contamination occurred on a Monday.

In October another case appeared. The study of risk factors pointed to a nurse specialist responsible for maintenance of health care equipment. At her home, in her shower, investigators discovered a jar of beauty cream she used every Sunday evening. It contained the notorious bacteria, which, while incapable of attaching to her skin, had succeeded in clinging to the nurse's false fingernails. Once the jar was thrown away, the epidemic ended.

In another anonymous hospital, again in the United States and again following cardiovascular operations, another type of bacteria that normally does not attack humans caused a series of infections. The epidemiological investigation identified an experienced nurse who was always present in the operating room during the surgery of the patients who were subsequently contaminated. The investigators questioned her. They discovered she had 25 cats, hosts to the bacteria in question, again transmitted by artificial fingernails.

These are just two typical case histories. Dozens more have been studied.[62] Elaine Larson has spent years fighting for nurses to keep their nails trimmed short, and against the use of false ones or nail varnish, three measures known to reduce the risk of infection. Nevertheless, when the Geneva Model came into general practice throughout the United States, the nurses' unions complained that alcohol ruined nail varnish and caused false nails to come unglued.

Didier was taken by surprise. "Nurses don't wear false nails!" he cried. He couldn't believe it was true. For him, it was as reckless as drunk driving. This unworldly man has always found certain aspects of human nature to be baffling. And other objections were raised in the U.S. The firemen came to the rescue of the American nursing unions. "With all this alcohol in the hospitals, you're going to increase the risk of fire." Didier wanted to bang his head against the walls. Imagination knows no bounds when it comes to finding that smallest thing that might halt change in its tracks. "I'd forgotten the degree to which alcohol was a sensitive topic in the United States," Didier explained. "Prohibition has left its mark." He suggested carrying out new studies.[63] The result: alcohol is of course inflammable, but the extra quantities needed in hospitals would not increase fire hazards.

In the end, however, nothing seems to prevent the spreading use of alcohol, promoted by this man who does not like its taste. Even hospital administrators have failed to distract him from his mission. When they claim they lack the funds to buy handrub, he advises them to eliminate antiseptic soap.[64] "And you'll actually have more money. At HUG we've saved between 20 and 24 million Swiss francs per year. It's a win-win situation." The studies corroborate Didier's assertions. They show that the adoption of alcohol is effective in terms of cost as well as public health.[65] Opposing this measure means opposing the common good. "I don't understand these people who give priority to economics over health."

Today, alcohol is winning the battle against soap, and even against false nails and varnish. When a new technology eventually comes along to replace handrubs, no doubt that too will arouse a wave of distrust. In the beginning, most actors in the medical community refuse to consider changing their ways. They need to be helped individually to regain control over their lives. That is the Pittet method for promoting hand hygiene.

CHAPTER IV

THE MULTIMODAL APPROACH

In 1998, Didier Pittet accompanied his protégé, the jovial Stephan Harbarth, to the United States, in the hope of finding a hospital willing to host him. During their tour, Barry Farr received them in Charlottesville, Virginia. "Didier, would you be willing to give us a talk?" As always, Didier agreed. He presented the Geneva Model, still in the process of development. "I was addressing the best team in the U.S. They bombarded me with questions." Two months later, Barry was distributing alcohol in his hospital. "He'd understood everything, or almost." But after an experimental period, Barry could detect no improvement in compliance. In an article, which revealed a certain perspicuity, he blamed the failure on his haste.[66] "We need to emulate Pittet," Barry concluded.

So what was the Pittet method? At the beginning of 1995, Didier needed to convince the personnel at HUG to adopt the alcohol-based handrub concocted by William Griffiths. He did not imagine even for a second simply pushing the change through. At the age of 37, he was still a young service chief. No one would sign him a blank check. "At that point, I thought of Pécub," he recalls. "He was an old friend. Before my departure for Iowa City, we'd worked together on a project for a comic about catheter infections. I thought we might try something similar with hand hygiene."

Pécub, or Pierpaolo Pugnale, a philosopher of communication, always brimming with ideas, suggested a different approach. "He'd just drawn a calendar for the Roche laboratories in Basel," explains Didier. "It concerned accident prevention. Every month, their employees would flip to a new drawing. For example, February focused on skiing accidents. So Pécub suggested putting up posters on the walls of the different services."

Didier went to find André Jacquemet, HUG's head of logistics and one of the hospital's big bosses. "He took a great liking to me." Didier spoke to him of his idea for a promotional campaign on hand hygiene and Pécub's proposal. Jacquemet suggested: "You should contact my son, he's a psychologist at the university and interested in how people change their habits. He knows which methods work, and which don't. He can help you."

When he recounts this critical moment, Didier once again mentions how lucky he was. "One, I had William, an alcohol expert, at my disposal. Two, there was Pécub, who gave me the idea about posters. Three, I met André Jacquemet's son, Stéphane."

During the course of his visit to HUG, Stéphane Jacquemet explained that in order to induce a change in behavior, you needed a multimodal approach. To get people to use seatbelts, for example, it wasn't enough to simply install them in cars. You needed explanations, police involvement, and promotion. Didier was easily convinced. He came up with a five-pronged attack.

1) Changing the system: make alcohol available as a substitute for soap. *Someone offers us a new car, without requiring us to use it.*

2) Training and education. *Someone explains how the new car is driven.*

3) Regular measurements and reports on rates of compliance and infection: creating a "feedback loop", as psychologists call it. Research shows that the better we're informed, the more we tend to comply with instructions, without it being necessary to apply fines or penalties for non-compliance.[67] *We need to know at what speed we're actually driving, in order to have a chance to adjust that speed to the authorized limit.*

4) Reminders and promptings through Pécub's posters and other communication tools. *Reduce your speed.*

5) Firm support from management to promote a culture of patient safety. *The government should help finance the new cars, agree to the installation of road signs, and encourage initiatives.*

At HUG, Didier created a "performance team" which met every month to make decisions collectively. *The automobile drivers themselves are the best placed to write the Highway Code.*

Barry Farr neglected the last three points. During his initial trial in Charlottesville, he believed that changing the system would be sufficient, forgetting the human factors. As Semmelweis's misfortune demonstrates, a brilliant idea does not bring about a lasting change if it isn't promoted properly. Change cannot be imposed. It must be adopted by each of the hospital's services, by each health care worker. "I also apply the Pittet method," sums up Valérie Sauvan. "I never order anyone to do anything. I never talk down to people. I keep a low profile. I make factual observations, without ever being critical. I've never had problems with anyone."

2

In April 1995, Didier called together the doctors and nurses for a plenary assembly in HUG's large auditorium. "I had enormous institutional momentum behind me. That was essential." He reported the results of the study carried out at the end of 1994. "That was our initial snapshot. We knew the degree of compliance and the infection rates. Now all we had to do was improve our performance." To set the tone, some of Pécub's drawings illustrated the presentation. Chubby characters with a few hairs sticking up out their heads, and in the background a hospital in flames where germs are running around. A doctor forgets to cleanse his hands before treating a patient, but remembers to do so afterwards. The caption was harsh: "Before, it's for him, after, it's for you." Compliance was indeed always better after contact with a patient. Protecting oneself comes more naturally than protecting others!

"We soon felt like we were coming under attack," recalls Marie-Noëlle Chraïti. At the time, this intensive care nurse had not yet joined Didier's team. She relates how Pécub's posters caused controversy. "It wasn't easy, being constantly called into question. The multimodal approach is great, but Didier ran into obstacles." To his face, everyone acted as if they supported Didier, but behind his back, there were moans and groans. "His enthusiasm crushed everything before it," says Francis Waldvogel. "Sometimes we had to pick up the pieces."

The posters were everywhere, in frames daubed with broad brushstrokes reminiscent of crisscrossed white bandages.[68] It was impossible to pass by without seeing them. They looked like patches meant to save the health system. The metaphor grafted itself to people's minds. The walls were starting to speak.

"We had to replace the posters twice a week to vary the messages," explains Didier. He needed good will on the part on everyone. One day, at four o'clock in the morning, he met with the hospital's cleaning staff as they were finishing their rounds. It was the first time a professor had ever come down to see them. Didier explained the object of the campaign and the value of hand hygiene. He received rousing applause. "We'll make sure your posters are pasted up." Pécub drew more than 250 of them. In one, a doctor is seen plunging headfirst into a vat of alcohol. The caption reads: "After the examination, decontamination!" In another, five hairy viruses are laughing together in bed. "If your hands aren't clean, here in bed we get mean!" One more advised "Trim those nails, or we germs set sail!" above a hand whose fingers resemble rocket launchers.

Didier arrived in his office one morning just as the telephone rang: "No, Pittet, this poster goes too far, you must take it down right away!" growled a man with a strong African accent. The image put up the night before showed a bacterium coming out of a coffee machine, with the caption: "There's no break for a small [cup of] black." During their monthly meeting in the tenth-floor cafeteria, the performance team had approved this poster. No one had seen any racist implications in it. "The important thing was to react quickly in such cases," Didier says. The following day, another image appeared. Two doctors are shaking hands, while gluttonous microbes jump from one to the other. The caption read: "Transfer of power." Or perhaps it was a surgeon in green scrubs, getting ready to draw his two guns to blow away a virus. "Disinfection, it's right there in your pocket!" A reminder to everyone to carry a bottle of alcohol-based rinse or gel on their person at all times.

People started writing on the posters, expressing their grievances: "You watch while we work." But there were also touches of humor: "More Valérie, less *bactéries*." Pécub developed a theory: it was hospital street art. "You should let it happen, you should even encourage it." He created new posters with spaces left empty for comments, and then went round the various units. His hidden motive was to spend time with the nurses, whom he adored. He questioned them and turned their messages into images, indicating the service where the idea originated at the bottom of the poster. "Pécub liked to foster team pride." The doctor coming out of the men's room zipping up his fly: "Did you remember to clean your hands?" retorts to another doctor, fleeing from an infected zone with black streaks trailing behind him, "In your shoes, I wouldn't talk!"

Pécub's posters stimulated discussion, but made people uneasy. The hospital workers continued to complain. To appease them, Valérie Sauvan went to see Didier's sister, Ariane, a painter and professor of fine arts. "I was very impressed when I faced this woman who was much more mature than me, splendid and renowned. She put her students to work on hand hygiene. We exhibited their work in the hospital, keeping them on the walls for a long time. I asked the technical service to help me hang them. It was really nice. I had the feeling I was doing ten different sorts of job, and enjoyed all of them. Everyone was accessible. If you wanted funding, you knocked on the door of the person responsible, and you came out with a budget. The program worked because the hospital itself worked well."

After two weeks on vacation, Valérie returned to HUG. She saw a deformed image of her face on the walls. "Didier is going to kill me. What did I do wrong now?" She went up quietly to her service. "It was a joke played on me by Sylvie. She's very good at those." Sometimes, there was tension among the nurses with their strong personalities, each of them seeking to outdo themselves; but no one ever lost sight of the pleasure of working together.

Every six months, Didier reported the results in the big amphitheater. When he announced that nurses performed better than doctors, cries of joys were met with whistles. Then he compared the different hospital units. Another explosion of cries. "Everyone played the game," Didier says. "There was a fantastic degree of competition. Lots of people came to the performance team's meetings with ideas. Each of them was adapting the strategy in order to better implement it."

One day, excessively happy with the campaign's success, Didier jokingly suggested that from now on they could fill the sinks with ice to stock cans of soda there. Implying they no longer served any useful purpose.

"Many people were shocked," says Marie-Noëlle Chraïti. "Didier likes to be provocative." On the other hand, she is unable to remember when she herself switched from soap to alcohol. She's not alone in this. "Despite everything, it all happened quite smoothly."

The campaign worked all the better because self-interested individuals cleansed their hands to protect themselves, while altruists did it to save lives. Doctor Jekyll and Mister Hyde both had their reasons for complying. The individual rubs elbows with the collective, and perhaps that is a necessary condition for widespread change to occur. We have a hard time acting on behalf of the planet because we generally don't see any immediate benefits in doing so. Things look different, however, once climate imbalances affect us directly. We're finally starting to link the personal and the collective. And hand hygiene has that rare power of uniting the two sides of the human coin.

"Didier faced all kinds of difficulties in carrying out what he considered to be a mission. Whereas Semmelweis was a revolutionary, Didier is a missionary," concludes Marie-Noëlle Chraïti.

3

Making a gesture as simple as cleansing one's hands into an historic innovation certainly requires a special kind of personality, a connection to people and to the most ordinary ideas, an open mind combined with an innate goodness. All of these are qualities can be traced back to childhood.

When Didier was born in March 1957, Robert and Fernande were living in a tiny apartment, which they soon exchanged for a quiet house in Petit-Lancy, opposite their electrical shop. Robert was quiet, reserved, very traditional and devout. For her part, Fernande found fulfillment in community work. They spent much of their free time involved in the activities of the Christ-Roi parish. On long weekends, they climbed up to La Fouly, an Alpine village perched at 1,600 meters at the end of Val Ferret in the Swiss canton of Valais, where a generous donor had bought a bankrupt hotel in order to turn it into a cooperative summer camp. The site offered an unobstructed view of a glacial valley, and there were immaculate meadows bordered by rows of pine trees. It would have been almost idyllic if the hotel's roof had not been threatening to collapse. The whole place needed to be renovated. Robert persuaded his artisan friends to pitch in. Fernande busied herself in the kitchen. Didier, soon joined by his sister Ariane, then his brother Denis, and a host of other children, played in the fresh air of the Valais mountains.

When the camp of La Fouly opened in the summer of 1962, run by volunteers from Petit-Lancy, Didier was one of the first to join. The priest led them on hikes.[69] He instilled them with a love of physical activity, making the stronger children walk behind the weaker members of the group, so that everyone would reach the summit at the same time. Caught up in this dynamic, Didier became an altar boy without even thinking about it. On Wednesdays, there was catechism. On Saturdays, boy scout meetings. Together, the children played soccer, went to summer camp, sang during Mass. On days when there were funerals, the parish priest would pick up Didier from school to participate because he didn't giggle during the service. The curate had him read the sacred texts. A recruiter, he raised the possibility of Didier starting religious training at a Catholic minor seminary following primary school. Fernande had no objections, but it was too far away from Petit-Lancy and Didier preferred to go to school with his friends.

Several years later, when Didier's godfather, his father's older brother, decided to become a Benedictine monk, Didier accompanied him to Tamié Abbey in the Savoie region of France. In this austere building on the heights overlooking Albertville, he woke up in the middle of night to attend the morning service, praying silently and singing the chants. He shivered as he watched his godfather walk away, called by God, but did not follow him.

He was friends with the son of his family's doctor. Didier spent a lot of time in the home of this quiet man, who was always ready to respond to an emergency, even for the hundredth time on a Sunday. Didier sensed a profession, a vocation, a calling there. At Tamié, Didier chose his destiny. He loved people too much to devote himself exclusively to God. Another path beckoned to him. Rather than a minister of souls, he would be a healer of bodies.

And so he found himself a quarter of a century later, with his pilgrim's staff, roaming through HUG's services, preaching hand hygiene. But soon the World Health Organization would be knocking on his door, and he would be travelling all over the world, motivated by the same faith.

4

In 2000, by the age of 43, Didier had become an authority. Benedetta Allegranzi, a young Italian woman specializing in infectious diseases, was one of his students. Three years later, back in Geneva for a six-month mission at the WHO, she was working on resistance to antibiotics. "It was at that moment when the first outbreak of SARS took place."[70] This type of pneumonia, caused by a coronavirus, emerged in China and spread across the planet during the spring of 2003. "I was transferred to the team monitoring the infection because SARS involved a high rate of nosocomial infections. I was dismayed. The WHO lacked the resources to fight it."

Benedetta didn't dare contact Didier who was working only a few kilometers away, on the opposite shore of Lake Geneva. She felt bad due to her helplessness. "I was too ashamed," she confesses with emotion. At the end of her mission, she returned to Verona, where she learned that a small amount still remained of the funds released by the Italian government for use by the WHO. "I proposed organizing an international conference on patients' safety. During its 55th World Assembly in May 2002, the WHO had voted a resolution on this subject without taking any action. Everyone agreed this was important, but nothing had been done since then."

The conference took place in Venice, Italy in April 2004.[71] There Didier met Benedetta again, along with colleagues and WHO officials. The minutes of the discussions reached Sir Liam Donaldson, the Chief Medical Officer for England, a member of the WHO's executive board and an expert on patients' safety. "He's a magnificent person and physician, a surgeon by training who later became involved with public health, someone really well-qualified," Didier says with enthusiasm. "A fine man. He was putting together a crack team to tackle the problem. He'd sent his spies to Venice. In a way, it was Benedetta who made it all happen."

Joining Donaldson in this effort were Donald Berwick, who later became President Barack Obama's administrator for Medicare and Medicaid; Lucian Leape, author of the seminal article "Error in Medicine";[72] Dennis O'Leary, head of the Joint Commission on Accreditation of Healthcare Organizations in the United States; and James Reason, a risk theorist and inventor of the "Swiss Cheese model": accidents occur when several causes converge, or metaphorically speaking, when several holes in a piece of Swiss cheese become aligned.

In October 2004, Donaldson and his team announced at a ceremony held in Washington D.C. the creation of the World Alliance for Patient Safety.[73] They knew that improving the planet's health care situation would take years. They envisaged setting a challenge every three years in order to motivate the medical community. "To head up this project, we needed a leader who was scientifically renowned and respected," Donaldson explains. "I knew of Didier's work in Geneva. He was the ideal person to turn to for help."

Donaldson went to see Didier at HUG. "We spoke for an hour. Didier was overflowing with energy and ideas, but remained humble and respectful of others. I left his office convinced that he was the right person to head up our first Global Patient Safety Challenge." When Donaldson called him back to propose that he take charge, Didier accepted on one condition: "First of all, I need three years to evaluate the burden of disease worldwide." He was afraid that he might have overlooked some risk factors. He wanted to measure the scale of the problem before putting the best strategy in place. He was thinking of intolerances, of allergies.

But Donaldson was categorical: "It's 2004, and you have to launch in 2005. We can't afford to waste time." Didier realized what he was really saying was: "It costs more to measure infections than it does to prevent them." Even so, he consulted with Sir Iain Chalmers, the father of systematic studies on health systems and founder of the non-profit organization, Cochrane Collaboration.[74] He was a scientific researcher noted for his rigor. Didier deplored the fact that no large-scale study of hand hygiene existed. "Donaldson is pressing me to make an early start." Chalmers looked at him with a faint smile. "In this field, we don't need any more studies. Go on, just do it."

Didier started by adjusting the multimodal strategy so that it could operate in any health care establishment. Speaking directly with each and every hospital director on the planet was out of the question! "We needed tools so that everyone could implement the strategy themselves," Didier says concisely.

He remained true to his pacifist approach. Never impose anything. Offer the possibility of change. Educate and incite. Hope that it comes about of its own accord. Dictators try to control everything; pacifists share their dreams with the community. Dictators impose a single path; pacifists show there are several different paths. They stretch the strings of their harps in the hope that a polyphony played by millions of hands will arise.

The WHO was lacking in means. The 16 million patients who were losing their lives every year to nosocomial infections did not weigh heavily in the balance.[75] Despite its urgency, this battle was of little concern to politicians. Didier very quickly received proof of this. He did not even have funding to hire a communication agency to create a poster explaining how to cleanse hands properly. So he consulted his oldest son, Florian, a student at the École Cantonale d'Art de Lausanne (ECAL – the leading Swiss school of art and design). "He came up with the idea of showing the gesture from the point of view of the person who performs it. He positioned himself above us while we cleansed our hands and photographed us. Using these photos, he drew our hands, decrypting all the gestures, step by step." On a shoestring budget, with the help of his colleagues at HUG and the WHO's support, Didier was ready to launch the program with full fanfare on 13 October, 2005.[76]

Before the big day arrived, he'd lost ten kilos in weight and was taking sleeping pills to make sure he got some shuteye. He walked up to the WHO's podium with disheveled hair and hollowed cheeks. He tried to forget the fact that Brigitte had just left him and draw from his inner reserves the enthusiasm needed for the forthcoming battle: treating all of the world's hospitals. His personal problems mattered little compared to the suffering of millions of victims of nosocomial infections. "You are the dream team!" he called out to the delegates who had come from the four corners of the world. "Better hygiene means better treatment. Clean hands are safer hands."[77] Didier had picked up his pilgrim's staff. "Some simple gestures can save lives. Every patient has the right to live."

CHAPTER V

AN ECONOMY OF PEACE

In January 2006, accompanied by Sir Liam Donaldson, Didier made his first trip to Africa as a WHO delegate. Leaving Geneva helped take his mind off his problems. He'd spent the holiday season brooding about his personal situation, while Brigitte moved into an apartment nearby. His life was going to pieces. By devoting himself to the welfare of others, he'd neglected to look after himself. He felt devastated. Séverine comforted him with her text messages.

Together they had organized the launch ceremony at the WHO. "She draped two immense banners down the ten floors of HUG's façade. She did a tremendous PR job for us." When he arrived in her office, she asked him if he was feeling all right.

"Yeah, yeah…"

"Are you sure?"

"Not really, my wife just left me."

The text messages kept alive this relationship that had not yet gained enough strength to awaken Didier's enthusiasm. In the meantime, he clung to his calling, even though it had already caused him to neglect his marriage and family. Rather than change his ways, he preferred to fight fire with fire, vaccinating himself with his work.

Together with Donaldson, they were driving back to Nairobi after visiting three Kenyan hospitals. They were two hours ahead of their schedule. Didier did not relish the thought of spending them alone in his hotel room. "How about making another visit?" Donaldson agreed and their driver took them to the Kijabe Hospital.[78] "Working for the WHO is great. Even unannounced, we're welcome everywhere we go. And in this case, once again there was another extraordinary turn of events. We went into a room and right away I saw, on a wooden stand under padlock, an alcohol dispenser."

In 2006, the hand hygiene program had been announced, but was not yet being implemented. The WHO was still selecting pilot sites.[79] They needed to be followed closely, and then recommendations based on their experiences would be written up, which would help hospitals all over the world to develop their own programs. That day was still far off, Didier was astonished to discover an alcohol-based handrub dispenser in a Kenyan hospital room where he'd turned up by mere chance.

He asked the nurse on duty when she used the alcohol and was delighted to learn that she knew at least some of the five key moments for hand hygiene. But the presence of the padlock bothered him. The alcohol should be readily available. Any hindrance would only limit compliance. "How much do you pay per bottle?" asked Didier, thinking that only expensive products would be placed under lock and key. The nurse didn't know the price and referred him to the hospital director.

On the way, Didier ran into Peter Nthumba, the hospital's chief surgeon, who had trained in Britain and returned there every three years for an update. On these visits, Peter would meet with former colleagues and they would take him to the operating room to show him the latest techniques. In 2003, the British campaign for hand hygiene was underway and Peter had discovered the use of the alcohol-based handrub. Upon returning to Kenya, he'd asked his director to buy some bottles. "Well, that explains the presence of alcohol where I wasn't yet expecting to find it," Didier noted with satisfaction.

He congratulated the surgeon, and then the director. "And how much do you pay for these bottles?" The director consulted the accounts and finally announced the price. "But that's scandalous!" Didier said angrily. "That's terrible!" The Kenyans were paying three or four times more for the alcohol than in Europe or the United States. When he left the hospital, Didier exploded. "The pharmaceutical companies are messing with us." He'd been on bad terms with them ever since his article in *The Lancet*, criticizing the gels they were distributing in Britain. "The price shouldn't be an obstacle for hand hygiene. If a preventive measure is costly, it won't work. The handrub has to be as cheap as possible."

The conclusion was obvious.

"They should produce it locally."

"That's a good idea," Donaldson assured him.

"We'll call it the 'WHO formulation for hand hygiene' and publish it everywhere. We'll break their stranglehold over the market. Then they won't be able to make profits at the patients' expense."

2

It was Didier's third big intuition. After realizing that soap and water weren't working, and that only a multi-modal approach would bring about change, he decided he needed to give the world the handrub formula and its five-point use protocol, for free. "Didier is a born humanitarian," says Donaldson. "He would never have accepted seeing the poor treated without proper hygiene."

After concocting the simplest and least expensive formulation possible, including one variant with ethanol and another with isopropanol, he established a WHO team which included, among others, Sasi Dharan, a microbiologist from HUG; Manfred Rotter, an expert in testing alcohol-based solutions; Syed Sattar, a specialist on their efficacy with respect to viruses; and of course, the indispensable William Griffiths.

"For William, it wasn't always easy," Didier observes. "It was if we'd torn his child from him. Every time we suggested a change, for practical reasons or cost, he had trouble accepting it. He was defending the ideal position of a chemist, while we were seeking to create a universal formula. But once again, his role was decisive. Industrial alcohol isn't necessarily pure. William came up with the idea of auto sterilizing it by adding hydrogen peroxide. That allowed any spores present to be killed."

In the end, the WHO team proposed two formulationss along with a production manual.[80] The first was composed of 80% ethanol, 1.45% glycerol to protect the hands, and 0.124% hydrogen peroxide, with the rest made up of water. In the second, ethanol was replaced by isopropanol dosed at 75%. Any less isopropanol or ethanol, as one sometimes finds in general use products sold in pharmacies or supermarkets, and the formulation is not as effective, or even useless.

Although both these recipes proposed by the WHO conform with European Union Standard EN 1500, they are in theory less effective than other more expensive formulations, such as the one originally perfected by William Griffiths for HUG, which included chlorhexidine, a patented product.[81] Nevertheless, they are highly reliable, and the WHO strongly encourages their adoption for at least five reasons:

1) They have a wide spectrum of action, and very few microbial agents resist them.

2) They are ideal for areas without sinks or access to clean water.

3) They increase compliance with hand hygiene by making the operation quicker and more practical.

4) Their cost does not exceed 1% of that entailed by lower compliance with hand hygiene. In most countries, a 100 ml bottle can be produced locally for less than 0.50 U.S. dollars.

5) They minimize the risks of secondary effects due to the high level of skin tolerability. "I prefer to use the WHO formulations," confides Marie-Noëlle Chraïti. "I find that they are less aggressive on the hands."[82]

On each of his trips abroad, Didier explains how pharmacists can make the new formulations locally for almost nothing. The key is the alcohol, which can be distilled from a large variety of plants. In Africa, it can be derived from nuts, maize, manioc, or sugarcane husks. Elsewhere, potatoes or beets can be used. Foreign pharmacists have started coming to HUG for training, such as Loséni Bengaly from the Point G Hospital in Bamako, Mali. Then they go home to launch their production chains and train their colleagues.[83]

"The pharmaceutical companies hated me." He's appalled by their greed, their blindness as juridical entities to individual suffering, their antagonism towards the common good. The missionary has awoken within him. He wants to eliminate every obstacle that stands in the way of his great work. He has understood that hand hygiene will only propagate itself if nothing hinders it, whether this be due to religious belief, or political and economic interests.[84] The formula had to be made public and available to all, like Newton's laws of gravity or a mathematical theorem. It had to be made part of humanity's heritage without anyone being able to place it under an embargo. The general interest had to prevail over special interests.

Didier does not consider himself to be making a heroic gesture. He is simply a doctor, doing what's best for the health of his patients. He forgets that in similar situations many other researchers file patents in order to reap personal profit. Pharmacies are filled with their innovations, often unaffordable to most people. Didier does not think like them, he does not understand them. He doesn't even criticize them. "Hand hygiene is something too simple, too necessary, for it to be patented. The idea never even occurred to me." Yet during a speech, he announced that if he took a tenth of a cent for every bottle of alcohol-based handrub solution sold throughout the world, he would earn 1.7 billion dollars per year.[85] His boss at HUG promptly declared him the most expensive doctor on the planet, due to the loss of revenue he cost them.

"The WHO had already made public the formula for rehydrating badly nourished infants," Didier explains.[86] "Before that, it cost a fortune. Now you just need a little cola, some sugar, and salt... and everyone can make it." According to him, he's simply following the long line of humanitarians before him. It's impossible to make him see that alcohol-based handrubs are destined for far more widespread use than the rehydration formula, that they're on a whole different scale.

Meanwhile William Griffiths points out that if the cantonal hospital of Fribourg had not released the original formula back in 1976, nothing would have come of it. The HUG team was only able to improve on it because it was free from the very start. Following on from that, at Didier's instigation, the WHO has been pursuing the same policy. "If the formula hadn't been free, Didier would have been held hostage by one pharmaceutical company or another. He would have been perhaps unable to meet the independence criteria demanded by the WHO. He would have been accused of a conflict of interests. The hand hygiene challenge never would have been launched."

3

Without knowing it, Didier has joined a political movement born at the beginning of the 1980s and spearheaded by Richard Stallman. At the time, this 27-year-old computer programmer was working at the Artificial Intelligence Laboratory at the Massachusetts Institute of Technology. The new central printer furnished by Xerox had an unwelcome tendency to jam up with paper. Annoyed, Stallman devised a way to modify the program managing the printer, not to prevent paper jams—which were caused by a purely mechanical problem—but to alert users whenever they occurred.

The trouble with this was that Xerox had not supplied the printer's source code. It was a black box. When Stallman learned that an engineer at Carnegie Mellon possessed a copy of the code, he went to visit him. The conversation was brief. Stallman was denied access for legal reasons. The code was protected by copyright. Stallman felt betrayed. For years, ever since the pioneering days of computing, programmers had shared their creations, modifying them, and remixing them like bricks in a Lego game. More often than not, they did not even bother to sign them.

"A program would develop the way a city develops," says Stallman nostalgically. "Parts would get replaced and rebuilt. New things would get added on. But you could always look at a certain part and say, 'Hmm, by the style, I see this part was written back in the early 1960s and this part was written in the mid-1970s.'"[87]

This system of intellectual capitalization was finally shattered at the beginning of the 1980s. Commercial secrecy and the hunger for profits undermined the spirit of cooperation. Sam Williams eloquently sums up the situation: "Like a peasant whose centuries-old irrigation ditch had grown suddenly dry, Stallman had followed the ditch to its source only to find a brand spanking-new hydroelectric dam bearing the Xerox logo."[88]

In Kenya, Didier discovered another kind of dam. Since the pharmaceutical companies imported the products in small quantities and were subjected to high customs duties, they were supplying alcohol-based handrubs at prices that were far too high and ended up making a technically abundant resource scarce.

"It was my first encounter with a nondisclosure agreement, and it immediately taught me that nondisclosure agreements have victims," says Stallman. "In this case I was the victim. [My lab and I] were victims." Moral victims in the case of computer software with a protected code, physical victims in the case of an essential pharmaceutical formulation.

Ever since then, Stallman refuses to sign nondisclosure agreements. He makes his code public instead of locking them up in a safe. In 1983, he founded the Free Software Foundation, an association with the goal of developing software whose source code would be free and form part of humanity's common heritage. The free culture movement was born.

In a similar manner, at the beginning of the 1990s, Tim Berners-Lee unleashed the World Wide Web and Linus Torvalds gave us Linux, an operating system that works with most Internet servers. They gave no thought to enriching themselves, but instead they have enriched us collectively. It's often said that their generosity was only possible in the digital world, which is an immaterial world. Didier proves to us that such gestures can be applied to health and to the human domain. His work takes on its full meaning with the prospect of a profound economic change.

At the end of the 1990s, members of the Free Software Foundation started to label free software as Open Source. In 2001, Creative Commons extended the idea to all works of the mind, whether they were technical, scientific, or artistic in nature. For a growing number of activists, it became obvious that there were two opposing strategies: either creations would be liberated, or they would be protected by restrictive copyrights.

"Do I share my ideas or do I privatize them?" innovators must now ask themselves. "Do I develop them myself, or do I permit all people of good will to develop them at the same time as me?"

In the old economy, these questions made no sense. When you had an idea, you couldn't really communicate it unless you made a big hit and became famous for earning billions by engaging successfully in economic warfare. Today, with communications technologies, we can transmit our ideas, our innovations, explaining them and accompanying them, before even making a business out of them.

Didier adopted this pacifist philosophy, spurred by a moral necessity: the determination to defend patients at all costs from nosocomial infections. This higher imperative led to an immediate economic consequence: since alcohol was abundant, it could not be privatized. For activists, the argument does not stop at this point. They generalize it: nothing that is abundant can be privatized. Anything that can be given away without cost should be.

This political stance should not be confused with communism. Following the professor of economics and information Nick Dyer-Witheford at the University of Western Ontario, it's been called *commonism*, in reference to common goods, or the commons.[89] Commonists are concerned with the harmonious management of common goods. They are both ecologists, worried about the use of rare resources, and open sourcers in the tradition of Stallman, involved in sharing abundant resources.

Commonism is the ethics of sharing. That which is limited should be economized and shared by all, as a common good. In the same way, that which is unlimited should be multiplied and shared by all, as a common good. Didier is a commonist in both senses. He's concerned with a rare common good, life, and with a potentially abundant good, essential medication.

When he decided during his visit to Kenya in 2006 that he would offer the formulation and the five-point multimodal approach to the WHO, Didier was not aware that he had discreetly entered the political arena. He was doing what seemed fair to him, but his gesture has contributed to a growing groundswell. The old culture of dam builders will be replaced by a gift culture, a culture based on an economy of peace. "You no longer have any reason to come kill me, in order to take what I've already given you."

Until now, entrepreneurs have enriched themselves within the framework of the predatory economy, and then, like Bill Gates, they may become philanthropists. Today, new men and women are renouncing wealth altogether. They share the fruits of their labors as soon as the opportunity presents itself. They refuse war, even an economic one. Their pacifism is a precondition to any action they take. Offering humanity the formula for hand hygiene cost only the price of posting a page on the WHO's website.[90] The gift culture develops alongside the information society. So it's very natural for the work of Didier Pittet and his team to be linked with that of Richard Stallman.

Yet this still isn't understood, despite everything. One morning, Stephan Harbarth burst excitedly into Didier's office: "Look what I just found. They're trying to patent your brain. An American company wants to appropriate the five-point multimodal strategy." Didier was flabbergasted. He'd never paid much attention to the issue of patents. "My nest, my home, is my hospital, my team. That's my family, and it's normal to share with it."

For many people caught up in the predatory economy, such generosity is not self-evident. Accompanied by an armada of lawyers, they attempt to seize what has been given. "It's disgusting. They won't get away with it. Our findings have been published by the WHO, by *The Lancet*, and even by Wikipedia." But one can draw some ominous lessons about human nature from this episode. Today, Didier is more famous for the fortune he gave up than for the millions of lives he saves each year.

4

At the end of 2006, Didier received a call from the British embassy. "I'm very moved," stammered a man whose voice Didier did not recognize. "The Queen wants to make you a knight of the Crown."

Didier burst out laughing, thinking someone was playing a prank on him.

"I'm quite serious," continued the man who introduced himself as the British ambassador to Switzerland. "I'm calling you from Berne to find out if you will accept this honor. The procedure has been underway for a year. We already have agreement from the Swiss ministries of Foreign Affairs and Internal Affairs."

The ambassador's emotion was so intense that it deeply touched Didier, who was struck by the solemnity of the moment. He accepted the honor, of course. When he learned that two nobles had nominated him, he thought of Sir Liam Donaldson, and perhaps Sir Iain Chalmers. He was stunned by the news, nevertheless. His friends all teased him. "It's such a British thing." Irene, his younger daughter, exclaimed: "Just Iike Paul McCartney, the old man from The Beatles!"

"Better," Didier jokingly replied. "In 1965, McCartney and the other Beatles were made MBEs, Members of the Order of the British Empire, whereas they're making me CBE, Commander of the British Empire, a higher rank!"[91]

The Queen officially named Didier a Commander on the 1st January 2007. The ceremony took place in Geneva in the company of his family, his friends, and his closest collaborators. As Didier was about to leave, the ambassador whispered to him: "You should have the medal insured by Lloyds. It costs a lot of money. Upon your death, your family will have to return it."

Once again, the ambassador seemed deeply moved, as if the entire weight of an age-old tradition rested upon his shoulders. Didier walked off to hide his own emotion. He thought of his sister, Ariane, absent that day, hospitalized due to a cancer. When he returned to HUG, he was greeted by cheers. "Put the medal on, put the medal on!" He took the medal out of its box. A chubby Genevan grabbed it out of his hands and put it around his own neck. "Take your pictures, guys!" he shouted, strutting around. An Englishman who was a member of the infectious diseases team came up to him. He seemed so furious that the crowd fell silent. "How dare you clown around like this?" He turned to Didier: "You shouldn't take this lightly."

Didier had no desire to laugh. He was well aware of the honor that had just been bestowed upon him. "For the British, this was really something important." He helped them set up the service for the prevention of infections at Hammersmith Hospital in 1999, and then offered them his advice during the launch of the national campaign for hand hygiene in 2003. He had given the formula to the WHO in 2006, and he'd always turned down monetary rewards, but he could not refuse the recognition. In an economy of peace, respect is all that binds men together. The extravagance of the symbol matters little.

"I've never seen anything quite so horrid-looking," Ariane dared to comment when Didier went to see her in hospital. "Turquoise, gold, orange, red... what an awful combination of colors." Very gaunt and bald due to chemotherapy, her skin a shade between yellow and gray, Didier's sister found the strength to smile. The painter and art professor might not have liked the look of the medal, but she was proud of her big brother. In her heart, she knew that he'd received the only kind of reward that really mattered to him.

Like Richard Stallman, Didier does not refuse awards. As opposed to money, recognition and thanks have the property of being available in unlimited quantities. They are the currency of abundance, the currency that irrigates the economy of peace. Money, on the other hand, is scarce. It creates inequalities, separating the rich and the poor. It arouses greed that sometimes proves fatal. But honor can't be seized, it can only be earned by the giving of one's self.

Of course, to be able to give, one needs to live in a protective ecosystem that satisfies basic needs. As a civil servant living in Geneva, Didier enjoys good financial security. Giving away the handrub formulas and their use protocol has not placed him in a precarious position. An economy of peace can only thrive in a framework that promotes mutual aid. Richard Stallman and Linus Torvalds are researchers, whose work is now sponsored by universities or non-profit foundations; Tim Berners-Lee was employed by the European nuclear research institute, CERN, when developing the world's first website.

Didier repeatedly says that he has always needed institutional backing, pointing out how, with its seal of approval alone, an intergovernmental agency like the WHO can lift mountains. Government is the system that allows individuals to satisfy their hunger, to house themselves, to have their illnesses treated, and to obtain an education. Government provides the minimal shell from which an economy of peace can emerge. Government must ensure the abundance of everything that can be abundant. Alcohol-based handrubs along with culture, information along with freedom.

On the other hand, when government acts to protect the dam builders, those who limit abundance, it strays from its mission. Bankers prosper from the scarcity of money, politicians from the scarcity of power, energy producers from the scarcity of energy. An economy of peace will not be generalized until each of these bottlenecks is eliminated one by one. So government itself will be transformed. It will no longer be the place where power is exercised, but where all people of good will cooperate.

"Everybody comes out ahead," Didier says delightedly. The pharmaceutical companies ended up congratulating him too. They even set up their own association for patient safety, called POPS, under the umbrella of the WHO.[92] "The consumption of alcohol continues to grow. They lowered their price, but their revenues are increasing. Even at HUG we signed up with a pharmaceutical company. Our in-house pharmacy no longer has time to produce the bottles we need. In 2012, we consumed 20 times more than in 1993-94." But when an institution cannot find a suitable supply of alcohol-based handrubs, it can synthesize its own. "In Malaysia, three companies controlled the market. It isn't a country with a high cost of living, the products were not expensive but they still involved costs, so the government decided to make them in a central pharmacy. The same choice was made in Hong Kong. Elsewhere, companies phoned us to ask permission to put on the packaging: 'WHO alcohol-based handrub for hand hygiene.' It was a great victory over the market."

By releasing the formula, Didier gave institutions the power to say: "No, not at that price, not with that formulation." He increased the hospitals' freedom with respect to the pharmaceutical corporations. No more patents. No more exclusive rights. The manna was shared equitably between all of the actors involved. Abundance has pacified a sector of the market to the greater benefit of the patients. It's an example that can be followed in other domains such as vaccinations or antibiotics.

CHAPTER VI
WORLD HYGIENE

When the H1N1-type virus appeared in Mexico in March 2009, epidemiologists knew that one of its cousins had caused the Spanish flu pandemic in 1917-18, which killed 50 million people. The WHO formed an emergency committee. "Didier, your alcohol, will it work in this case?" asked Margaret Chan, the organization's director-general.

"H1N1 is an encapsulated virus, like all flu viruses. It's easy to destroy."

In May, the WHO's annual world assembly was supposed to be held at the Palace of Nations in Geneva, with all of the health ministers present.

"Should we cancel this meeting?" wondered Margaret, who was worried about infection at a gathering of people from all corners of the globe.

"There's no need to do that," Didier reassured her. "Let's distribute a HUG kit to all 3,000 guests. Each of them will have a face mask, detailed information on protecting oneself from viral infection, and a bottle of alcohol-based handrub with its use protocol."

There was no panic yet, but in June the WHO went to a level 6 alert, declaring the outbreak to be a pandemic. The distributors of alcohol-based handrubs seized the opportunity to put their bottles in all the supermarkets, and even hardware stores. "You went to buy a saw, and came back out with an antibacterial gel." The labels clearly indicated that disinfecting one's hands helped to fight against H1N1. People were starting to stock up on provisions as if it were wartime. Pharmaceutical corporations had their production lines running 24 hours a day. Soon the supermarkets were sold out of their stocks. When buying her newspaper at a tobacconist's shop, Didier's editorial assistant, Rosemary Sudan, saw bottles of HUG's handrub on sale at ten times their cost. "Somebody was stealing from us."

Hospitals themselves came close to running out. Didier had stern words for the pharmaceutical companies. "You can supply the supermarkets, but you supply the health care institutions first." It was only common sense. H1N1 actually killed less than an ordinary flu, and thousands of times less than nosocomial infections, the invisible pandemic. Nevertheless, everyone became aware of the need for hand hygiene. In the hospitals, compliance increased. People became frightened for themselves.

"It was because of H1N1 that alcohol entered the wider community. Perhaps if I hadn't offered those bottles to the WHO assembly, nothing would have happened. There were dozens of journalists on hand, so they didn't go unseen. It got outside the hospitals because of me." In a way, the H1N1 virus helped spread the idea of hand hygiene. It became the vector, just as the MRSA epidemic of 1992 had opened the doors of HUG's services to Didier's teams. A biological vector had in a sense propagated a "cultural virus" alongside it. It implanted within us the means of fighting the disease it caused.

Henceforth, the world population is ready to listen to the advice of doctors in cases of a major health risk, but Didier remains uneasy. "I just don't know the five moments for hand hygiene in the case of Mr. and Mrs. John Doe. I haven't carried out the studies." The codification of the five moments within hospitals required years of research.[93] Immense databases were cross-checked. "I have done nothing similar with respect to the wider community. I don't want to be dishonest."

When one insists, Didier ventures to give some advice. After going to the toilet. Before preparing a meal. Before and after eating. After sticking a finger in one's nose. After shaking hands...[94] "It's just common sense, but common sense isn't scientific. I'd need to create a whole foundation," he says with shining eyes, "but without money, that's impossible. I don't have the team for that. The WHO has never been rich. Since 2008 and the subprime financial crisis, it's almost in a state of bankruptcy. Millions of people will pay for the damage done."

Thanks to his research, Didier helps save millions of lives every year, but he lacks the resources to pursue his investigations. The benefits would be gigantic for each of us but he's not in a position to generalize hand hygiene outside of the hospitals. "If hand hygiene improved in the community, we'd have fewer infections and we could prescribe fewer antibiotics. That's another health time bomb right there. By prescribing antibiotics so often, we're creating resistances and we're making the world population more vulnerable.[95] Hand hygiene is the best means of limiting the use of antibiotics. It's a way of attacking the problem at the root. Quite simply by reducing the reservoir of infectious diseases."

Fewer colds and fewer flu cases means fewer days off sick at work and at school, and lower spending for health care systems. We would all have something to gain from that, in terms of well-being and financially, but governments are not sufficiently committed, while private companies have no interest in investing in an economy of peace. Fewer ill people would mean less revenue as far as they are concerned, so universal adoption of hand hygiene would probably not increase their profits.

"At home, I never clean my hands with alcohol," explains Didier. "Soap is no doubt adequate. We would just need to know with certainty the opportune moments, and then launch a multimodal campaign in the community." But it's still too pacifistic an initiative to be implemented. Didier obviously dreams of it, however.

"It's my absolute desire, but it's not enough to say: 'Here are the bottles of alcohol, use them as much as you like.' No, the message is: 'Hygiene in general is crucial, and hand hygiene is the most important thing of all. When you go to the hospital, you play a part, so that patients there receive better care. And when you're at home or in a public place, you can also play a part."

2

Hand hygiene is almost too good of an idea. If countries such as France are exemplary in their efforts, making the use of alcohol a criterion of health care quality,[96] others are more lax, starting with the United States. Having taken the lead in the 1970s and 1980s due to the zeal of lawyers, they then lagged behind in response to that same zeal. The best way to avoid lawsuits was to neglect measuring infection rates. Out of sight, out of mind. That meant one of the five elements of the multimodal strategy was missing: the reporting of results. All too often, U.S. health care workers do not know the real rates of infection in their service and have no means of knowing whether their performance is improving or not. In these conditions it's difficult to correct or improve behavior.

"In many states, such as Michigan, health insurers no longer cover the cost of hospital stays when patients have a nosocomial infection," Didier says in an outraged tone. "If you're a doctor, you have less and less reason to declare them. Soon, urinary infections, the most common kind, will not be covered by insurers at all!"

Didier then provides an alarming outline of medical history:

1) The existence of nosocomial infections was unknown.

2) The medical profession learned to recognize them.

3) It started to prevent them, notably with hand hygiene.

4) They were perceived as an indicator of poor quality care.

5) It was therefore decided not to cover the costs entailed.

6) From a strictly material point of view, it was better not to detect and record them at all.

7) So, with a wave of the magic wand, they disappeared, and we're right back where we started.

The discourse of the anti-hygiene camp encourages this downward slide. In some cases, it easily corroborates Godwin's law,[97] by assimilating present-day hygienists who are solely concerned about public health with the racist hygienists of the Nazi period. Other critics observe that children from rural areas are less ill, and above all, less allergic than children living in urban areas. They assert that growing up in the country, despite exposure to animals and other sources of microbes, is therefore healthier than the sanitized cities. The real reasons for this phenomenon no doubt lie in urban pollution, induced stress, and the lack of open space. "I would advise all these skeptics to go for a cruise along the Nile during a diarrhea epidemic," Didier comments angrily. "It's *ca-ca-clysmic*. Then they can come back and tell us that hygiene is harmful."

To convince oneself that such claims are unfounded and open one's eyes to medical reality, one only needs to compare the causes of mortality in different regions of the world. In countries where hygiene is difficult to implement, infections are the major cause of death.[98] Hygiene doesn't promote infections, it saves lives.

"We're never too clean," Didier insists. "To be sure, hygiene-related illnesses do exist. Women who wash too often can develop vaginal problems or suffer from eczemaWomen who wash too often can develop vaginal problems or suffer from eczema. Apart from these very rare cases, I've never seen complications with people who wash too much. But with those who don't wash, I have seen them, many times. The truth is cruel: people are less clean today than our grandparents were. They were more aware than us of the dangers of poor hygiene. Since we're ill less often than they were, we pay less attention, and then we start making up absurd theories. In the cafés, because people don't wash their hands when they go to the toilet, we find urinary bacteria in the peanuts."

Didier returns to scientific facts. "One idea underlying all this retrograde discourse, which is absolute groundless, is to say that if you disinfect your skin too often, you'll wind up replacing natural skin flora with another. That's quite false in the case of alcohol. We've proved that it protects the native flora.[99] It only kills bacteria at the surface and does not prevent those at deeper layers from continuing to live and migrate towards the surface. No imbalance whatsoever has been demonstrated." To sum matters up, alcohol eliminates the transitory bacteria that arrive from the exterior. It does not carry out any selection of the microbial flora on the surface of the hands. "Mind you," Didier warns, "I'm against living in an asepticized world. At home, you need to keep things clean, not disinfect everywhere. But to claim that we should avoid an excess of hygiene, especially when caring for patients, borders on absurdity and is even dangerous."

Hygienism—the promotion of good hygiene—is even regarded by some as a new form of dictatorship, as denounced by Bénabar in his song À notre santé (To Our Health):

They lead a life without excess,
Keeping a close eye out for every vice,
Having a perfect body is a sacred duty,
But their health capital is worth the price.

He drinks beer without alcohol,
She avoids meat due to cholesterol,
They drink their coffee decaffeinated
With sweetener that's not sugar-tainted.[100]

The critics forget that we now forbid smoking in public places to prevent a minority of smokers from poisoning non-smokers, by virtue of a simple ethical principle: my freedom stops where that of others begins. This collective hygiene measure does not affect what happens in a private setting. Hand hygiene is a social hygiene. "You do as you please in your home, but in public you respect the freedom of others, starting with their health."

In the name of liberty, some people may mock this principle. They can assert their own right to be ill, but they should understand that the great majority of people don't feel free when they're confined to bed, and even less when they risk dying due to stupidity. In a collective context, freedom is necessarily constrained.

Hand hygiene is a simple way of eliminating physical suffering and also a form of elementary politeness, like not blowing smoke in the face of one's neighbors. So it's a gesture of social pacification, under the same general heading as an economy of peace.

Didier is loath to venture further into this terrain. He does not want to see accusations being made, such as: "You didn't clean your hands, and you've contaminated me." He has never published studies of compliance with people's names attached. For him, anonymity remains essential. It's up to each individual to make their decisions with full knowledge of the facts. Nothing is ever imposed. No practice is ever stigmatized. One simply repeats the message as parents have always done: "Wash your hands, it's good for you." And now one can add: "It's good for others, too."

Semmelweis preached zero tolerance. He sought to eliminate nosocomial infections in his maternity clinic. Didier is not quite so idealistic. The more medicine becomes complex, the more the risk of infection increases. And similarly, the more we travel. To help us resist better, Didier does not support absolute hygienism, but looks for scientific evidence and collective practices that would be beneficial for us. He prefers to prevent rather than cure, to act before rather than after. In some respects, he has an almost Asian way of thinking.

Traditionally in China, doctors were paid only as long as their patients remained healthy. If illness struck, they were to blame for not having known how to avoid this. Didier advocates hand hygiene, vaccinations, and any other measures that might prevent risks. He's like an electrician who installs circuit breakers, so that power overloads don't cause fires or burn out the relays. He's looking out for the health of humanity.

3

Francis Waldvogel, Didier's mentor, is full of praise for his former student. "He's gifted when it comes to big projects. And he was already gifted when it came to producing very good clinical studies. He has a knack for them, along with a quality that I've almost never seen elsewhere. Reading his papers, I often find myself thinking that I would never be able to write them." But he hedges these remarks and refuses to place Didier at the top of the list of some forty professors that he first discovered and trained during the course of his career. "On a purely scientific level, his work is probably inferior to that of some of my other students, who have more brilliant scientific track records than his."

Didier himself agrees with this assessment. All he's done is follow in the footsteps of Semmelweis.[101] With, nevertheless, a truly extraordinary result: millions of lives spared each year. One would probably need to go all the way back to Sir Alexander Fleming, the discoverer of penicillin in 1928, to find a doctor who has played an equally determinant role. The scientific work of Didier, of William Griffiths, and of the entire HUG team, matters because of its immediate practical impact. The Cartesian side of our nature sometimes ignores this dimension. We often attach more importance to things that are difficult to conceptualize and generalize than to those which concern well-being or the community. In a way, we're too intellectual, favoring reason over the body. This expresses itself in an almost innate propensity to value the predatory economy over an economy of peace, an economy belonging to the quantitative order rather than one based on quality.

Yet, in the medical domain, and more broadly speaking, in politics, ideas are not judged in the laboratory but out in the field. Didier was delighted when Lule Haruna announced that he'd massively reduced nosocomial infections at his 100-bed bush hospital in the heart of Uganda.[102] No one had obliged him; he achieved this out of professional conscientiousness with the aim of improving his patients' well-being. "It only takes one motivated person to change the situation in a country."

In Johannesburg, South Africa, Didier visited one of the most modern hospitals in the world. "They've followed the WHO program to the letter." He then crossed over a hill and, ten minutes later, found himself in another hospital that exists in a state of extreme poverty. In the immense inner courtyard that serves as an emergency room, several ill people die each day due to the lack of adequate triage during admission, the simplest cases and the most serious ones being mixed together. Didier was appalled. Apartheid may have been abolished, but he was discovering its last lingering effects. When he entered the intensive care service, he noted that the doctors were making their own alcohol. For once, he was unable to feel enthusiasm about this, even though, deep inside, he thought it was a small step forward and probably indispensable for greater changes to take place.

In Iran, he introduced the nurses working in the Public Health service to the protocols for preventing infections. Three years later, there are 900 of them involved with hand hygiene, measuring and preventing nosocomial infections day after day. "That's more than in Switzerland. It's normal for me to compare the situation with my own country. Iran is doing better than Switzerland. They have a national campaign to monitor their hospitals. At home, our hospitals manage on their own. Some of them do nothing!"

In China, with his friend, Professor Seto Wing Hong from Hong Kong, Didier visited centers of traditional medicine. "If it has existed for thousands of years, it's because it works. There, it is the patients who cleanse their hands. As a sign of respect for their doctor." Seto's assistant, Patricia, adapted the five moments to this ancestral practice.[103]

1) Before touching a patient (hands-on examinations are universal).

2) Before performing an aseptic gesture, especially when using acupuncture needles.

3) After the risk of exposure to a biological fluid, even if traditional medicine is not very invasive.

4) After having touched a patient.

5) After having been in contact with a patient's environment, it's indispensable.

Everywhere Didier goes, out in the field, he leads the fight in close proximity with the patients. Medicine does not always progress by way of laboratories, theory, and abstraction. It forms part of a struggle for human dignity, day after day, never ceasing.

So Didier travels the world, rallying countries to the WHO's program. It's never easy to acquire a signature. Sometimes, he has had to hunt down the health ministers concerned. In France, it wasn't possible because elections were approaching, and then because they had just ended. The signature finally took place by video conference. In China, it was postponed at the last minute. The contracts needed to be renegotiated and two years were lost before an accord was finally reached.

In Japan, Didier required several stays before managing to resolve the situation. When the Japanese sign something, they honor their commitments, whatever the cost. After eating a traditional meal during which he was fed *fugu* cleaned of its own poison, Didier succeeded in reassuring the three ministers in charge of health: "We're not asking you to achieve zero tolerance, but simply to join up with us." It's through partnership that things advance.

In Cameroon, in September 2008, he had 27 African ministers all signing at the same time. On other occasions, he grabbed hold of ministers at the WHO's annual World Assembly in Geneva. "You're helping us to grow up," the Swedish minister confided to him. He meant humanity, and each of us within that humanity. "In Western eyes, we may not seem very realistic," the health minister from Bhutan declared. "We belong to those nations working for a common movement of the universe. So we want to participate in your project."

Didier had tears in his eyes. The minister had just put into words the feelings that have always motivated him. A sort of wave that has carried him, and us along with him, towards greater harmony. He never dreamed of such a handsome reward. He set into motion a dynamic which he no longer controls. The small seed planted in a HUG service has now given birth to a planetary forest. Beyond their religious, political, and economic divergences, the peoples of the world can agree on using alcohol-based handrubs. Hand hygiene has become world hygiene. Today, it has led to a global entente, and undeniable approval on all sides.

4

On 11 October, 2012, a journalist from the French M6 television network came to see Didier. Under the eye of the camera, Didier told him all about hand hygiene and then they visited the hospital. Didier took him to intensive care and introduced him to the heads of the service, notably its boss, Laurent Brochard, a world expert on non-invasive respiratory assistance. Nurses paraded in front of the camera.

"Do you think Professor Pittet should have filed a patent?"

"You don't know Professor Pittet. He never would have done that."

The questions continued, and Laurent Brochard came over to see how matters were proceeding. The journalist took the opportunity to interview him. Didier moved away to give them some space. As always, hospital staff members were bustling in the corridors. The journalist went back to Didier.

"I have one last question. What would you do if you received the Nobel Peace Prize?"

"Excuse me? Are you joking?"

"You're on the lists."

"No one knows who's on the lists," Didier replied, refusing to rise to the bait. But in a corner of his mind, the thought occurs to him: *A Nobel prize would mean the possibility of creating a foundation and of developing hand hygiene in the community.*

When the journalist left, Laurent approached him, brimming with excitement: "What's this I hear? It seems you're going to receive the Nobel Peace Prize."

"It's just a rumor."

The following day, the Nobel committee awarded the 2012 prize to the European Union "for having over six decades contributed to the advancement of peace and reconciliation, democracy and human rights in Europe." Didier will have to wait. But one can already imagine his citation: "For having contributed to popularizing hand hygiene, reducing nosocomial infections by half, and permitting nearly eight million lives to be saved each year."

This exploit goes beyond medicine. It involves raising self-awareness concerning the risks inherent in our gestures, and thus immediately leads to an awareness of others, of their environment, and of the world that surrounds them. One can entertain the idea that through paying greater attention to our hygiene, a sort of intimate ecology, we will extend this attention to the entire planet. It would be futile to promote hygiene in a biosphere that has been abandoned to pollution and a predatory economy. One can only conceive of progress in this field within a pacified global context.

5

Didier wakes every morning at around 5 a.m. He answers the e-mails that arrived from America and Asia during the night and then goes down into his garden. He crosses the gravel bed, still a bit damp, follows the French-style garden path, and arrives at the four narrow bands of earth where he grows his vegetables. He enjoys this time of day before his thoughts grow restless. For the moment, his mind is still empty. He glances up at the menacing shadow of Mount Salève, bends over his tomato plants and tears away the suckers. He repeats these age-old gestures with a ritualized meticulousness. He joins with the men of yesteryear and of tomorrow. When an idea emerges, he pushes it back, keeping his distance from diseases, death, and dizzying eternity.

In the course of his daily communion with the earth, Didier steps out of ordinary time, this continuum dominated by unending exchanges, constantly accelerated by the slingshot effect of technology. He rediscovers how simplicity alone can change the world. Science revealed the power of alcohol. But right away, it fades into the background, leaving only two hands that interlace and momentarily rid themselves of pathogenic germs. This gesture gave rise to profound transformations because it transmitted itself from being to being, from heart to heart. So it propagates itself, spreads, and takes on life, animated by its own necessity.

But nothing can be taken for granted. Laurent Brochard, the chief of intensive care at HUG, had to resign due to a cabal formed by several senior colleagues on his team. The immediate result was that rates of nosocomial infections started rising again in the intensive care service. Hand hygiene works everywhere, in London and New York, in Kenya and Mali, but the slightest defection can hinder it, even in Geneva, the place where it all started. The gesture may very well be simple, but it requires constant attention. Administrative complications are enough to put it in jeopardy.

"I no longer have time for field inspections," admits Claude Ginet, in charge of the nursing service on Didier's team. "I'm buried in paperwork. That's true for all of us. To have a computer transferred from one office to another, I have to fill out a whole file and wait three weeks for the matter to be dealt with." Administrative tasks don't sit well with patient safety. They distract health care workers from the ordinary gestures, which nevertheless save lives. "How many times do nurses fail to disinfect their hands before taking a blood sample?" asks Claude. "If we don't keep after this, there's no follow-through. I've been hospitalized here myself, in a room with six beds. I saw things—and I said nothing. The nurses would have taken it the wrong way."

But if Claude says nothing, what patient would dare do so? "They want only one thing, to be back home. They're afraid of *doctors* and *professors*." Isn't that the heart of the problem? In almost every other domain within society, we don't use titles like *doctor* and *professor*. There's a vestige of the old class society within the medical world. This barrier needs to be overcome for hand hygiene to become an enduring habit, with all of us as it guarantors. This is the new mission that Didier has set for himself.

SIMPLE COMPLEXITY

1

When I sat down for the first time in the living room of Didier and Séverine, in their house at Croix-de-Rozon, only a few meters from the French border, right away I saw the complete works of Gandhi on the top shelf of the bookcase. I thought of the famous quotation often attributed to him: "Be the change you wish to see in the world."[104] After conversing for several hours with Didier, after questioning his colleagues, reading his scientific articles, exploring the Web in search of photos and videos, I found myself still thinking of this quote.

If I cleanse my hands, I change a corner of the world. Didier has armed me with an unalienable gesture, just as Gandhi armed me with another inalienable gesture, non-violence. I have all I need within me in order to act. And if we were millions, or billions, doing the same, then the change we would like to see in the world would come about. We don't need to ask for anything from anyone. We require no authorization. We don't need to wait for the next elections or overthrow the government. We are armed with our wills.

Everything begins with the gesture rather than the word. Because it is simple, we can appropriate it and repeat it. Through its constant multiplication, no doubt, a new civilization will spring forth.

Why not dream of this? If I am less ill, I will become less irritated and grumble less. I imagine myself being less violent and extrapolate from this a healthier society whose citizens would also be healthier. So would there be less crime, less corruption, fewer wars among nations? A surplus of education, a surplus of collective intelligence, along with fewer crises?

Because the gesture is simple, it can have unexpected, complex repercussions. This simplicity is even one of the necessary conditions for complexity, which is merely an intertwining of elementary interactions deployed almost infinitely. When starlings fly together in flocks they merely obey a handful of rules. The result is nevertheless prodigious: magnificent V, W, and other topological formations outlined against the evening skies of autumn when their migrations take place. Gandhi with non-violence and Didier with hand hygiene have given us a few simple rules which could, through their combinations, completely transform our lives and those of future generations. But unlike some engineer seeking to be all-powerful, let's not try to define this future in any great detail. Let's dream it, and then let it blossom. Like a flower, or like a child.

2

Yes, it's true that Didier did not invent anything, as I sometimes hear it said. He merely assembled the pieces of a puzzle. A new image emerged that no one had yet been able to see. Soap and water were not working. The system had to be changed, through the conversion to alcohol. But for that change to occur, a multimodal strategy had to be devised, meaning a strategy that supported change rather than imposing it. And in order to deploy it on a worldwide scale, the costs of producing the alcohol-based handrub had to be reduced by releasing its formula. From methodical observation in the medical field, this involved a radical shift towards more social, political, and universal issues.

At present, under the aegis of the WHO, the World Day of Hand Hygiene is celebrated every year on 5 May.[105] In health care centers across the globe, activities intended to heighten the awareness of personnel have multiplied. Videos of the hand hygiene dance circulate on Internet, with a resounding success for HUG's very own choreography, Ô les mains (Hands Up).[106] In this clip, you see male and female nurses taking their bottles of alcohol-based handrub, rubbing the top and the bottom of their hands, and then their fingertips, before putting the bottle away. They approach a patient. And they renew the disinfection gesture, over and over, between each therapeutic act. Suddenly, a female nurse halts the hand of a male nurse before he touches the patient. They exchange an explicit glance. After having manipulated some papers, he's forgotten to disinfect himself. Fluorescent germs seize the occasion and pass from hand to hand. The gesture that saves lives has to be carefully repeated once more. It has to be performed without thinking about it, out of reflex. And also performed at home, to protect one's loved ones. Performed at work, at school, in cafés, everywhere, because it's simple, because it's a sign of politeness, of respect, of peace.

"I come to you without contaminating you."

It's an assertion close in its intent to another, far older one: "I come to you without weapons," as warriors signified when they shook hands. It was a gesture of peace in a world at war, but also a gesture that is a vector for potentially harmful germs.[107] Why not replace it then with the *namaste* employed by Indians, joining both hands before one, and bowing slightly? The adoption of this gesture would be the logical conclusion of Didier Pittet's work. A gesture of peace in a world at peace.

ACKNOWLEDGEMENTS

Without Geneviève Morand, I never would have heard of Didier Pittet. She realized that my interest in an economy of peace could find nourishment in the story of hand hygiene. Without Didier's complete availability, without his openness and his welcome, along with that of Séverine Hutin, I never would have undertaken this work. Didier was the motor, arranging my interviews, asking his family, his friends and his colleagues to find time to see me. Thanks to all concerned. Benedetta Allegranzi, Laurent Brochard, Marie-Noëlle Chraïti, Sasi Dharan, Sir Liam Donaldson, Nicole Fichter, Claude Ginet, William Griffiths, Daniel Lew, Brigitte Pittet-Cuénod, Laure, Irène, Florian and Virgile Pittet, Miles and James, Robert and Fernande Pittet, Valérie Sauvan, Rosemary Sudan, Josiane Sztajzel-Boissard, Sylvie Touveneau, Francis Waldvogel. Thanks to lOurs and to Boel, my faithful first readers. Thanks to Lilas for her stimulating copy-editing. Thanks to my translators whose feedback helped me further improve the text: Thomas Clegg for the English-language edition; Fuzuki Mizuno and Pascal Durand for the Japanese; Claudia Arlinghaus and Gabriele François for the German; Elisa Reyes and Antoine Barral for the Spanish; Régine Ferrandis for the Portuguese. And special thanks to Suzanne Jamet, my editor at L'Âge d'Homme.

NOTES

1   Or the equivalent of a bottle in terms of administrative support, assistance, or the development of projects.

2   Translation by Stuart Gilbert (Knopf, 1948). First publication in French: *La Peste*, 1947.

3   The World Health Organization (WHO), whose headquarters is in Geneva.

4   Leishmaniasis is a chronic ailment which presents itself in cutaneous and/or visceral form, caused by flagellate protozoa belonging to the Leishmania genus. Transmitted by insect stings, this parasitic disease affects humans and numerous other mammals, with 2 million new human cases occurring each year.

5   It is difficult to obtain accurate figures. The best large-scale study of the incidence of nosocomial illnesses was carried out in 2002, in the United States ("Estimating Health Care-Associated Infections and Deaths in US Hospitals", *Public Health Reports*, March-April 2007). The four main causes of infection (involving blood, urine, the lungs, and surgical sites) represent half of all infections observed in hospitals (Zingg W, Huttner B, Sax H, Pittet D, "Assessing the burden of healthcare-associated infections through prevalence studies: what is the best method?", *Infection Control Hospital Epidemiology*, 2014). In 2002, healthcare-associated infections affected 1.7 million American patients and killed 5.8 % among them. According to a WHO study published in *Lancet* in January 2011 (Allegranzi B, Bagheri Nejad S, Comberscure C, Graafmans W, Attar H, Donaldson L, Pittet D, "Burden of endemic healthcare-associated infection in developing countries:

systematic review and meta-analysis"), these infection and mortality rates need to be at least doubled in non-Western countries. When these numbers are applied to the world population in 2013, the statistics become dizzying: each day more than 400,000 people are infected in hospitals, and 46,000 die from the consequences of these infections. In the West, nosocomial illnesses kill nearly 9% of all people, rising to 34% elsewhere in the world, for a total of 16 million deaths per year. They are far and away the leading cause of human mortality, ahead of heart disease and vascular accidents, which each year kill 13.2 million people. In wealthy nations, with 69 deaths per 100,000 inhabitants, they are ranked second, ahead of lung cancer and tied with vascular diseases. Better hand hygiene is reducing these numbers by half.

6   At the beginning of 2014, 133 member states of the United Nations are engaged with the WHO in the promotion of hand hygiene. More than 50 countries have launched their own national promotion campaigns.

7   New Influenza A (H1N1) is an acute respiratory illness which appeared in 2009. Transmission occurs in about half of cases by contact, either direct (for example, shaking hands), or indirect (by the intermediary of a contaminated surface), and in the other half by exposure to the airborne virus.

8   A parasitic disease affecting the liver. Human infestation occurs accidentally through contact with a parasitized dog. The parasite penetrates the intestinal wall and lodges itself in the liver.

9   "Concerns over treatment of infections", *The Globe and Mail*, 24 April 2013.

10 "Rita McNeil died of an infection she caught in hospital - Why & what to do", Robert Paterson's weblog, 26 April 2013.

11   If one goes back over the data provided in the 2002 study of American hospitals cited in note 5, the authors find about 99,000 deaths resulting from five major causes of infection. Assuming these represent only 50% of all nosocomial infections, one thus arrives at a figure of 200,000 victims per year. The Boeing 747-400 can carry up to 524 passengers, giving the equivalent of 381 crashes per year.

12   Michel Foucault, *The Birth of the Clinic* (Routledge Classics, 2003), p. 20. Translation by A.M. Sheridan Smith. First publication in French: *La Naissance de la clinique*, 1963.

13   Guillaume Depardieu & Marc-Olivier Fogiel, *Tout donner* [Giving One's All] (Plon, 2004).

14   "Golden staph" or *Staphylococcus aureus* is the most pathogenic species within the Staphylococcus genus, responsible for food poisoning, localized infections and septicemia – blood infections – during grafts or the placement of prostheses, for example.

15   See "French doctors face manslaughter charges", *The Guardian*, 24 December 2003, concerning the scandal over nosocomial infections in French hospitals, and mentioning both Guillaume Depardieu and Jean-Luc Lagardère.

16   We've taken the infection and mortality rates for the United States presented in note 5 and extrapolated them for France. With a population of 65 million in 2012, this gives us a figure of 770,000 infections per year (0.59% of the population) and 40,000 deaths (with a mortality rate of 5.8%). These figures do not take into improvements made to the introduction of alcohol-based handrubs. One can hope that the numbers have now been reduced by half.

17   Guillaume Depardieu & Marc-Olivier Fogiel, *Tout donner, op cit.*

18   The family of methicillin-resistant staphylococcus aureus (MRSA in English; SARM in French) is responsible for a

pandemic of infections affecting all the world's continents. The resistance of the staphylococcus to methicillin was identified only six months after this type of semi-synthetic penicillin was put on the market, in October 1960. Since the end of the 1960s the proportion of methicillin-resistant staphylococci has steadily grown, starting in hospitals, then spreading to the community at large, before becoming a global pandemic that has spared no continent, with the proportions of resistance sometimes exceeding 90%.

19 William RJ, "Bennett & Brachman's Hospital Infections", *Ovid*, 6 November 2013.

20 Pittet D, "Se faire soigner, ça rend malade ?", *Femina Forme*, October 2006.

21 "Epidemic of seasonal (2012-2013) influenza in a large teaching hospital" and "Nosocomial influenza prevention using multi-modal intervention strategies; 20 years of experience", *Antimicrobial Resistance and Infection Control*, 20 June 2013.

22 "The top 10 causes of death", WHO Fact sheet N° 310, July 2013.

23 See note 5.

24 The branch of medicine dealing with the internal organs in all their interactions.

25 www.lancydautrefois.com

26 Béris P, Audétat F, Beyner F, Pittet D, Jeannet M, Miescher PA, "Hautes doses d'immunoglobulines par voie intra-veineuse pour le traitement des neutropénies auto-immunes", *Swiss Medical Weekly*, October 1985.

27 Pittet D, Lew D, "Les infections liées aux cathéters intra-veineux", *Revue Médicale Suisse Romande*, 1988.

28 Didier Pittet and his colleagues in the United States were the first to quantify the importance of this phenomenon.

"Nosocomial bloodstream infection in critically ill patients: excess length of stay, extra costs and attributable mortality", *JAMA*, 25 May 1994.

29 Sax H, Pittet D, "Surveillance des infections nosocomiales : premier pas de la prévention", *Revue Médicale Suisse*, 26 April 2000.

30 "A semiquantitative culture method for identifying intravenous-catheter-related infection", *The New England Journal of Medicine*, June 1977.

31 "The efficacy of infection surveillance and control programs in preventing nosocomial infections in US hospitals", *American Journal of Epidemiology*, 1985.

32 "The emergence of methicillin-resistant Staphylococcus aureus", *Annals of Internal Medicine*, September 1982.

33 See note 26.

34 Frankart L, Copin P, Alexiou A, Henry N, Sauvan V, Pittet D, "Prévalence des infections nosocomiales dans un hôpital universitaire : distribution, facteurs prédisposants et indices diagnostiques", *Schweiz Med Wochenschr*, 1998.

35 Louis-Ferdinand Céline, *La vie et l'œuvre de Philippe Ignace Semmelweis, 1815-1865* (Gallimard, 1924). Translated into English by Robert Allerton Parker as part of: *Mea Culpa & The Life and Work of Semmelweis* (Little, Brown, 1937). But our translation herein.

36 This infection is caused by bacteria that penetrate the uterus and then are carried to the peritoneum and other abdominal organs.

37 Quoted by Louis-Ferdinand Céline. Our translation.

38 *Ibid.*

39 *Ibid.*

40 *Ibid.*

41 Hibiscrub soap was first introduced in 1960.

42 Pittet D, Mourouga P, Perneger TV, "Compliance with handwashing in a teaching hospital", *Annals of Internal Medicine*, 19 January 1999.

43 "Preoperative disinfection of surgeons' hands: use of alcoholic solutions and effects of gloves on skin flora", *British Medical Journal*, 16 November 1974.

44 These bridges are necessary for stabilizing the structure of certain proteins.

45 Larson E, Girard R, Pessoa-Silva CL, Boyce J, Donaldson L, Pittet D, "Skin reactions related to hand hygiene and selection of hand hygiene products", *American Journal of Infection Control*, 2007.

46 Sax H, Allegranzi B, Uckay I, Larson E, Boyce J, Pittet D, "My five moments for hand hygiene": a user-centred design approach to understand, train, monitor and report hand hygiene", *Journal of Hospital Infection*, 2007.

47 Boyce JM, Pittet D, "Guidelines for hand hygiene in healthcare settings", Centers for Disease Control and Prevention, 25 October 2002.

48 Pittet D, Boyce J, "Hand hygiene during patient care: pursuing the Semmelweis legacy", *Lancet Infectious Disease*, April 2001.

49 Touveneau S, Pittet D *et al*, "Alternatives au lavage antiseptique des mains et amélioration de l'observance. VIIe congrès National - Société Française d'Hygiène Hospitalière, Arcachon, France", June 1997.

50 Translation by Stuart Gilbert (Knopf, 1947).

51 Thierry Crouzet, *Les crapauds fous* [The Crazy Toads], 2014.

52   Harbarth S, Pittet D, Grady L, Goldmann DA, "Compliance with hand hygiene practice in pediatric intensive care", *Pediatric Critical Care Medicine*, October 2001.

53   Pessoa-Silva CL, Hugonnet S, Pfister R, Touveneau S, Dharan S, Posfay-Barbe K, Pittet D, "Reduction of health care-associated infection risk in neonates by successful hand hygiene promotion", *Pediatrics*, 2007.

54   *Ibid.*

55   See note 42.

56   "Impact of a prevention strategy at vascular-access care on incidence of infections acquired in intensive care", *The Lancet*, 27 May 2000.

57   Pittet D, Hugonnet S, Harbarth S, Mourouga P, Sauvan V, Touveneau S, Perneger TV *et al*, "Effectiveness of a hospital-wide programme to improve compliance with hand hygiene", *The Lancet*, 14 October 2000

58   Brown TL, Gamon S, Tester P *et al*, "Can alcohol-based hand-rub solutions cause you to lose your driver's license? Comparative cutaneous absorption of various alcohols", *American Society for Microbiology*, 28 December 2006.

59   Ahmed QA, Memish ZA, Allegranzi B, Pittet D, "Muslim health-care workers and alcohol-based handrubs", *The Lancet*, March 2006.

60   Kramer A, Rudolph P, Kampf G, Pittet D, "Limited efficacy of alcohol-based hand gels", *The Lancet*, 27 April 2002.

61   Passaro DJ, Waring L, Armstrong R *et al*, "Postoperative serratia marcescens wound infections traced to an out-of-hospital source", *The Journal of Infectious Diseases*, 2007.

62   "Artificial Nails and Healthcare Associated Infections", icpassociates.com, May 2004.

63 Boyce JM, Pearson ML, "Low frequency of fires from alcohol hand rub dispensers in health care facilities", *Infection Control Hospital Epidemiology*, 2003. Kramer A, Kampf G, "Hand rub-associated fire incidents during 25,038 hospital years in Germany", *Infection Control Hospital Epidemiology*, 2007.

64 John Boyce demonstrated the benefits of this in the United States: Boyce JM "Antiseptic technology: access, afford-ability, and acceptance", *Emerging Infectious Diseases*, 2001.

65 Pittet D, Sax H, Hugonnet S, Harbarth S *et al*, "Cost implications of successful hand hygiene promotion", *Infection Control Hospital Epidemiology*, 2004.

66 Muto CA, Sistrom MG, Farr BM, "Hand hygiene rates unaffected by installation of dispensers of a rapidly acting hand antiseptic", *American Journal of Infection Control*, 28 June 2000.

67 "Harnessing the Power of Feedback Loops", *Wired*, 19 June 2011.

68 www.hopisafe.ch.

69 For an account of this summer camp, see Abbé Willy Vogelsanger, *Une maison pleine d'enfants : L'histoire d'une colonie* (self-published, 2009).

70 Severe acute respiratory syndrome linked to the corona-virus. It appeared in China in November 2002, provoking a pandemic in May 2003.

71 Pittet D, Allegranzi B, Sax H, Bertinato L, Concia E, Cookson B, Fabry J, Richet H, Philipp P, Spencer RC, Ganter BW, Lazzari S, "Considerations for a WHO European strategy on health-care-associated infection, surveillance, and control", *Lancet Infectious Diseases*, 2005.

72 Lucian Leape, "Error in Medicine", *JAMA*, December 1994. He also published *To Err Is Human: Building a Safer Health System* in 1999.

73 "The Launch of the World Alliance for Patient Safety", Washington DC, USA, 27 October 2004. Official website: Patient Safety.

74 This association, cochrane.org, has the objective of organizing in a systematic fashion information concerning medical research.

75 See note 5.

76 The announcement of the launch was published in *The Lancet*. Pittet D, Donaldson L, "Clean Care is Safer Care: a worldwide priority", October 2005.

77 The official WHO website for the campaign is "Clean Care is Safer Care".

78 www.kijabehospital.org

79 The results of implementation at pilot sites in Costa Rica, Italy, Mali, Pakistan, and Saudi Arabia were published in August 2013 in *The Lancet Infectious Diseases* : "Global implementation of WHO's multimodal strategy for improvement of hand hygiene: a quasi-experimental study".

80 "Guide to Local Production", WHO, 2009.

81 They don't systematically conform with EN 12791. This European Union standard describes a test procedure simulating practical conditions in order to verify whether a product intended for surgical disinfection reduces skin flora sufficiently. It involves measuring the immediate bacterial decrease (where the WHO formulations achieve very good scores) and the effect maintained after three hours (where the WHO formulations score less well but without any real consequences because one needs to perform handrubs several times per hour).

82 Pittet D, Allegranzi B, Sax H, Chraïti MN, Griffiths W, Richet H and WHO Global Patient Safety Challenge Alcohol-Based Handrub Task Force, "Double-blind, randomized, crossover trial of 3 hand rub formulations: fast-track evaluation of tolerability and acceptability", *Infection Control Hospital Epidemiology*, 2007.

83 In 2011, a study showed that local production of alcohol-based handrubs was being carried out on a large scale: "Local production of WHO-recommended alcohol-based handrubs: feasibility, advantages, barriers and costs", *Bulletin of the World Health Organization*, 2013.

84 Pittet D, Sax H, Hugonnet S, Harbarth S *et al*, "Cost implications of successful hand hygiene promotion", *Infection Control Hospital Epidemiology*, 2004.

85 Didier Pittet announced these figures in a speech given in 2006. He based this calculation on the average consumption of handrubs by HUG in 2001-2002, which he then generalized to the whole planet by using the annual number of hospitalizations worldwide, estimated by the WHO in 2005 (723 million).

86 "Improved formula for oral rehydration salts to save children's lives", WHO, 23 March 2006.

87 Quoted in Sam Williams, *Free as in Freedom: Richard Stallman's Crusade for Free Software* (O'Reilly Media, 2002).

88 *Ibid.*

89 "Commonism", *Turbulence*, 2007.

90 WHO webpage: www.who.int/gpsc/en/.

91 The four Beatles received their MBEs in June 1965, but McCartney was elevated to a full knighthood in 1997 for his services in the field of music, thereby becoming officially Sir Paul McCartney.

92 Private Organisations for Patient Safety.

93 The WHO's five moments were officially published in 2007: "My five moments for hand hygiene": a user-centred design approach to understand, train, monitor and report hand hygiene", *Journal of Hospital Infection*, established after an article that appeared in *The Lancet Infectious Diseases* in 2006: "Evidence-based model for hand transmission during patient care and the role of improved practices".

94 See "The Fist Bump Manifesto" *The Atlantic*, 22 November 2013

95 "The Evolving Threat of Antimicrobial Resistance. Options for Action", WHO document, Patient Safety, 2012.

96 Ministère des Affaires Sociales et de la Santé, République Française, www.sante.gouv.fr/score-agrege.html See score ICSHA2. The volume of alcohol-based handrubs consumed is the second indicator listed in the table, following the composite indicator of activities to combat nosocomial infections.

97 Godwin's law: "As an online discussion grows longer, the probability of a comparison involving Nazis or Hitler approaches 1."

98 "The top 10 causes of death", WHO Fact sheet N° 310, July 2013.

99 "WHO Guidelines on Hand Hygiene in Health Care", Part I, Chapters 5 and 6.

100 In French, the song runs as follows: Ils mènent une vie sans excès / Font gaffe à tout et se surveillent de près / Avoir un corps parfait c'est un sacerdoce / Mais leur capital santé mérite des sacrifices / Il boit de la bière sans alcool / Elle mange pas de viande ça donne du cholestérol / Ils boivent leur café décaféiné / Avec du sucre dé-sucrifié

101 Pittet D, "The crusade against puerperal fever", *Lancet*, 2004.

102 Haruna L, "Gombe Hospital hand hygiene project", June 2013.

103 "Study on adopting the WHO 5-moment of hand hygiene for practices in traditional Chinese medicine (TCM) clinics", *Bio Med Central*, June 2013.

104 There is no documentary evidence that Gandhi used this exact wording. Gandhi did write the following, however: "If we could change ourselves, the tendencies in the world would also change. As a man changes his own nature, so does the attitude of the world change towards him. ... We need not wait to see what others do." in his article "General Knowledge About Health", first published in *The Indian Opinion*, 9 August, 1913; reprinted in *The Collected Works of M.K. Gandhi*, (The Publications Division, New Delhi, India), vol. 13, ch. 153, page 241.

105 "Save Lives: Clean Your Hands", WHO.

106 Hand hygiene dance - WHO/HUG, Geneva, YouTube, 2009.

107 "Reducing pathogen transmission in a hospital setting. Handshake verses fist bump: a pilot study", *The Journal of Hospital Infection*, 25 September 2013.

**Private
Organizations
for Patient
Safety**

This book recalls the challenge that is the fight against healthcare-associated infections, and how hand hygiene has transformed action that protects patients across the world. This book has benefited from the special support of bioMérieux, B. Braun Medical, Hong Kong Infection Control Nurses' Association, Laboratoires Anios, SARAYA, as well as POPS (Private Organizations for Patient Safety), a collaboration facilitated by the World Health Organization that aims to promote and support global patient safety. POPS companies supporting this book: B. Braun Medical, Deb Group, Ltd./DebMed USA, LLC, Ecolab, Elyptol, GeneralSensing, GOJO, Hartmann Group — Bode Science Centre, Laboratoires Anios, SARAYA, Sealed Air and Surewash.